NOSH!

THE INTERNATIONAL DIET COOKBOOK

FIRST EDITION

NOSH!
The International Diet Cookbook

FIRST EDITION

By

Liv Jones

Edited by Shannon D. Jones

ISBN: **978-0-578-05323-3**

www.noshcookbook.com

Dedicated to my lovely family;
Shannon, Chance, and Serenity
to whom I love more than a million Welsh cakes.

TABLE OF CONTENTS

Breakfast Recipes: Page 125

TOP 10 RECIPES

1. Double Chili Cheeseburger   68
2. Mojo Burritos   104
3. Liv's Lasagna   74
4. Breakfast Burritos   127
5. Banana French Toast   126
6. Poutine   135
7. Fat Free Brownies   157
8. Fast Food French Fries   61
9. Philly Cheesesteak   80
10. Pigs in a Blanket   77

(Picture: Stockel Market, Brussels Belgium)

NOSH DEFINED

NOSH (Noun) : [singular] \\'näsh\\
    1. Food.
    "The pub has great nosh."

NOSHING (Verb) :
    1. Eating
    "Noshing on a cheeseburger!"

NOSH UP (Noun) : [singular]
    1. A large satisfying, excellent meal.
    "That was a stellar nosh-up!"

POSH NOSH (Noun) : [singular]
    1. A fine, elegant meal.
    "He took me to the movies and then a posh nosh."

Etymology: Yiddish nashn, from Middle High German naschen to eat on the sly.

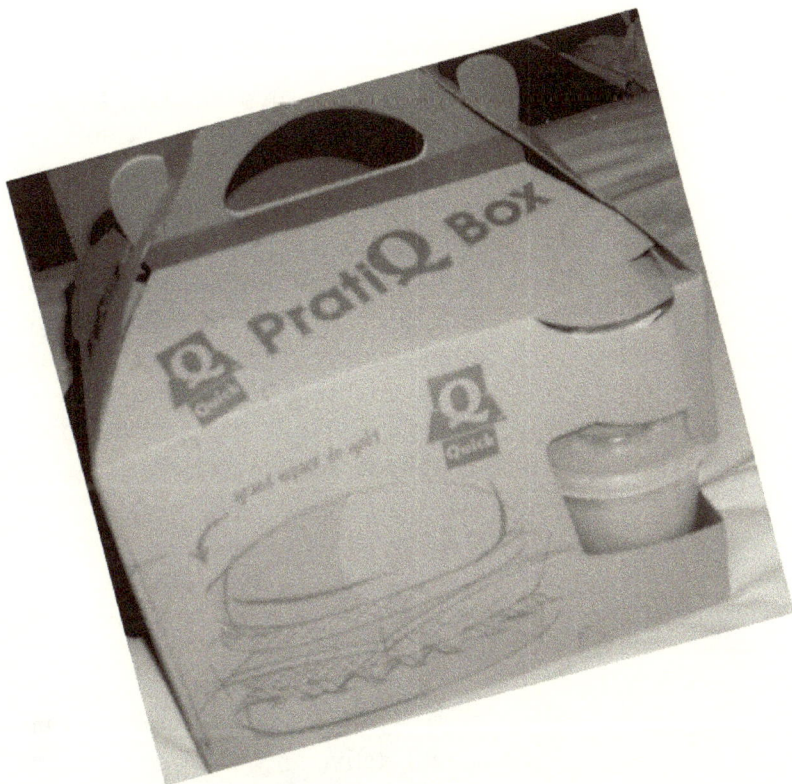

PREFACE

"Food is to life, as romance is to love.
It's the common social experience that silently shadows
life's every experience." -Liv

It was the love of food, I must admit. First I began
eating it, then eating too much of it, and eventually I found
a way to write about my love of food and make money
doing it. Writing fast food reviews and the comical
adventures which ensued in obtaining them was a great
deal of fun, but never very smart when it came to my
health. I couldn't just give it up, food that is... but
something had to be done, clearly I needed intervention...

Biscuitville
November, 2005

I'm always amused by the food we eat here in North Carolina. I'm reminded by that fact each time my relatives from California come to visit. We don't sleep in till 10 AM here. We don't skip breakfast. Here, in North Carolina; we pledge allegiance to our sausage biscuit every morning like some sort of patriotic salute to the pigs who died in honor of breakfast. Slap it between a flaky buttermilk biscuit, pour me a huge glass of sweet tea and drop some hash browns in the deep fryer. This is how the East Coast does breakfast.

Today it was Biscuitville that would deliver my U.S. government recommended daily fat allowance in one single meal. I drove up to the menu board, and surveyed the possibilities. Deciding what to eat is like Russian roulette, you know the gun has a bullet in it, you've been here before, but you gaze at the sign with a vacant stare trying to decide how to clog your arteries without keeling over in cardiac arrest. Biscuitville has four core ingredients that make up a plethora of menu items: eggs, biscuits, bacon, and sausage.

Genuine biscuit connoisseurs can increase their enjoyment by asking for double meat, double cheese, or carbohydrate naysayers can get their "healthier" CarbSmart breakfast which is merely a small bucket filled with meat and cheese. Not wanting to take the healthy route, I opted for the double decker sausage and cheese biscuit. Thankfully it's a part of their value menu, so when you order it you can just say, "I'd like a number one"- so you don't sound like nearly as much of a fatty. The lady in the speaker then asked me if I'd like to up-size it? My stomach is saying "Oh yeah!" My brain is saying "You're kidding, right?" I'm quite certain up-sizing is a beneficial sales technique for a company in the business of selling comfort food, but it's immature to give an overweight woman in the drive-thru extra grease and fat when she's already wheezing from cranking down the window to get her food. It's like giving an alcoholic a bottle of vodka, and handing them keys to a sports car. It's irresponsible. Let's be honest, no one should have that much food for breakfast unless you're a construction worker, a firefighter, or a superhero.

So I pull up to the window, look left, then right, and quickly slip them my Visa. The guilt begins. Like a crack addict at her dealer, part of my brain was saying "drive away Liv, drive away!" The other side had already given in. "Resistance is futile." I knew there was no turning back now.

The next few moments are a blur. Time slows down. "Ketchup, mam?" The smell of huge vats of frying oils, the bustle of people running to and fro in the kitchen.... "Thank you, have a nice day." Suddenly I'm lucid again, and exiting the drive-thru.

There, sitting before me is my steaming brown bag of food spewing its aromatic fumes like a smoke stack of sausage and cheese. I reach inside in an attempt to extract my biscuit from the bag. The size of the biscuit combined with the velocity in which I tried to remove it resulted in the oil saturated bag ripping and this massive object of lustful grease landing in my lap. There it was: a huge two story buttermilk biscuit, with twin massive patties of sausage that glistened with grease and cheese in the morning sun. For a moment I swore I heard a choir sing "Hallelujah!"

Due to the dangerous size of this biscuit I probably shouldn't have been driving down the interstate at rush hour. But *"hey"* I live dangerously. Every time I would go to take a bite of this monster, the sheer size of it blocked my vision as I drove down the road.

By the time I reached work I was so full, and so tired from the effort of eating all the food, all I really wanted to do is take a nap. But then I looked down and forgot it came with French fries. It was right about then I began talking to my breakfast again. "You have got to be kidding me," I asked?
The food didn't respond. When I arrived at work I shut the car off, and curled up in the back seat to take a siesta for the remainder of the day- but fifteen minutes later, my boss came knocking on the car window. I mumbled "go away" with little success. She opened the door, and shoved a cell phone in my face which was screeching my spouses voice and some rather unpleasant monologue with lots of yelling and several references to "intervention." I pulled myself together and made my way into the building, wiping off the crumbs as I walked. As I swiped my entry card I attempted to suck in the stomach but found it was too painful.

Sure, it was funny. It admit, but clearly it was obvious by everyone around me at that time in my life I should be admitted to Fast-Food-Anonymous and be dealt a large dose of electro-shock therapy to cure myself. Oddly, no one did, and I continued in my downward spiral of deep fried destruction...

McDonald's
Steak, Egg and Cheese Bagel
December, 2007

Despite the common consensus lately that no one under twelve years of age should go to McDonald's. I have to admit they do three things really well.

The Big Mac, the Fish Fillet, and the Steak and Egg Breakfast Bagel. The last of those three we will discuss here today.

If you're not familiar with McDonald's steak bagel, that's okay. It's a relatively new menu item appearing in the last five years or so. Apparently finding a way of inserting the human equivalence of cat-nip in a breakfast bagel took McDonald's engineers a while to figure out; but alas, they succeeded.

Let me describe this incredible sandwich to you. Take one bagel, and some sort of meat that tastes exactly like steak, but looks a little like a gray square hamburger, add sautéed onions, some cheese and eggs... and there you have it: McDonald's Steak and Egg Breakfast Bagel. Yummy!

The grease from the steak is like an au jus that soaks into the bagel just enough to give it that soft chewy taste. The joke's on you when your realize some technical genius put McDonald's greasiest food on a bagel- the very bread that has a hole in the middle of it to drain its drippings on your clothes.

Price wise it's unlikely you'll find any other restaurant offering steak and eggs for $3.95. Either the local steak house is price gouging or McDonald's loves its customers so much that they're subsidizing the cost. I can think of no other reason to explain the phenomenon. It is a true modern day mystery.

I decided to investigate. Yesterday while making my journey through the McDonald's Drive-thru, I asked the lady taking my debit card what kind of steak it was. "Whatcha mean what kinda steak it is?", she asked with a slight deflective tone.

I inquired, "Well is it a T-bone, a Porter House, a rib-eye?"

Her: "Uh, hun it's a McDonald's steak."

Me: "Oh, really. It does from a cow right?"

 Her: "Oh no, honey it comes from a truck that comes on Mondays."

I was now impersonating that one eye squint, sideways head thing, that my dog does when she's trying to understand the meaning of life. Right about then I could tell I was holding up the line when the guy behind me leaned out his window honking his horn and yelled "Are you ordering the whole freaking cow lady?" I looked in the rear view mirror with an evil glance to acquire whom might be making this rude remark, stuck my head back out the window and was about to reply with the quickest comeback I could think of when I noticed my drive-thru concierge had disappeared from her station, exited the back door, and was now screaming: "Tyrone I told you not to come around while I'm working."

The manager whom witnessed the stage-right exit, and subsequent vacant position, approached the drive thru window and apologized as she handed me my food while being partially distracted by the curious events occurring behind me.

I'm now smiling from the obvious unexpected comedy of the situation and without actively censoring myself properly commented to the now rubber-necking manager: "Maybe he didn't get his happy meal?"

It's at this point in the story, Liv comes to the realization that something has to be done. I had a great gig writing, was content and happy with my sedentary life, yet something was missing. I didn't feel healthy. I didn't feel I was living life. I felt merely as a passive passenger on the train of life, while the scenery kept passing by. I'm not sure why, but right about then is when I made the most important changes of my life. I gave it all up for something better. I learned what I'm about to tell you right now; that one does have the ability to control and change one's life, for a better life, a better me.

This is that journey.

Prologue

"The manifestation of one's own self is defined by no more or no less than what one is capable of imagining." -Liv

It's been about a year since I made the decisions that have led me to where I am today. On this journey I've found some unexpected surprises, pitfalls and possibilities. I always knew I wanted myself to be thinner, and healthier, but I've also seen my children and my spouse join me in this adventure and together we've lost more than 200 pounds. It also inspired me to start writing down all the new forms of baking and cooking we developed in order to get here. I really never anticipated that those recipes, and my concepts would become a book, but when people ask you how you lose weight, and you tell them "chili cheeseburger" or "burritos" and "brownies", people first say "No seriously?" Then they start asking for your secret.

The truth is there really is no secret. No magic genie in a bottle. All that's really needed is a change in perspective. Burgers, pizza, and my favorite family recipes- I can still eat them all. When I educated myself on how to cook with the right ingredients and methods something remarkable happened. Something I like to think of as food enlightenment.

That's what this cookbook, and my writing it aspires to accomplish. Rather than preach what or what not to eat- it is my hope to teach the reader through my recipes how to take their own favorite foods and create a better meal out of it. From the moment you opened the cover, I hope you realized that this isn't a cookbook or a collection of recipes and I'm not a chef; what you're holding in your hands is a metaphorical spark to light a fire. Ideas, which can lead to more than just food. This cookbook is but a facade for a training manual on survival in suburban cooking.

Along the way I hope you'll enjoy the culture and foods of my family and perhaps one of my favorite recipes will become one of yours.

"Very Good Grasshopper"

Everything in life has rules. Traffic laws for driving, etiquette in formal dining; even matter and energy must follow a set of rules called physics, or the reality we live in begins to break down. Even when we are educated and aware of the rules, and their consequences, in many situations as humans we often choose to break them, either intentionally or unintentionally. Sometimes we make our decisions because we fail to fully seek out the necessary knowledge that allows us to understand the importance of why the rules are there. Eating is no different. While we're not splitting atoms, and we've all heard most of this before, it's probably best we set some ground rules before we hit the ground running. So here they are, the first nine lessons of eating:

Fast Food:
Eat it occasionally. It should be less the 5% of your entire diet. Try to pick healthy options, and research menus before finding yourself in public without a clue.

Sugars:
As much as possible try to reduce your sugar intake. Using diet sodas, artificial sweeteners, light or sugar-free syrups when possible.

Carbohydrates:
Carbohydrates can be okay despite recent diet fads to the contrary, but you've got to know which carbohydrates. Whole grains should, when you can, be the obvious choice, and controlling your intake of white flour products can enhance weight loss.

Exercise:

I'm not talking running a marathon. Try parking your car at the far end of the lot from now on. Physical activity generally improves with diet, but it's definitely something you want to include as often as you can in your life. Just remember with both eating and exercise it's the little things that add up to big changes.

Learn:

As in, read the label on the box. It's that simple. Educate yourself every time you buy something. When you buy a product it comes with free nutrition information, why not use it?

Often you'll think one type of food labeled "healthy" is better for you when it's not. In some cases regular is less fat, and less calories than the "healthy" version. *Light* does not mean fat-free, and food manufacturers are in business to sell you as much food as possible, not make you healthy. Remember that.

Accept Failure:

It's going to happen. Accept it. If you're doing it right 95% of the time, then that 5% time when we're out with friends eating out or dining with family on comfort foods, then you'll still succeed.

Overcome the Fear:
Don't be afraid to try something new. I tell my children the mantra all the time, but often I had to remind myself in the process of changing the way I cook, often being happily surprised by the outcome.

Fear in general is huge cause of failure. Such as the fear of being hungry. Sounds silly, but we all do it. Sometimes I'll even try to convince myself because I've only budgeted $10.00 for dinner that I should buy a slightly fattier version of a food because it's cheaper, and that we'd have more food. In these moments of weakness I discover afterwards I feel nothing but guilt. What we've learned is that it's worth spending a dollar or so extra on the low-fat versions because down the road we won't be spending that money on diet drugs, or medical costs. We won't have to exercise that extra hour, and we won't be as likely to have our lives cut short by the choices we made earlier in our lives to merely save a buck.

Never go Hungry:
It's a simple concept. Your body will override your rational thought if you're hungry, and you have access to fattening foods. Whether this is fast food, or merely grocery shopping you're guaranteed to make the wrong choices, or buy too much food when you're hungry. So don't.

Break the rules:

It's okay. Not only do you need to accept that there will be days when you're going to eat badly and feel guilty about breaking the rules. I encourage you from time to time to do it. That guilt is what reminds us we still want to change. Have one too many slices of pizza every now and then! Gorge in your favorite fast food treat when you've had a crappy day and your boss is being a nutter! It's when you ignore that guilt after eating high fat food, or no longer feel badly about it, that you need to contemplate stricter guidelines. Screw up! Gain a pound! But then get back up off the ground, and start thinking for the next meal, *before* you're hungry. Eat smarter and get that pound back. You can do it!

Starting Over: Eating 101

Like a bad boyfriend it's time to move on. He's been abusive, and not just calling you fat, but making you fat. This is the new you, and here are foods that will make you fall in love all over again:

Meats:
Lean Meats are probably the most important part of losing weight. Unless you're willing to go vegetarian, (in which case you're probably not reading this) then meat will be the foundation of many of the meals you make. I've found myself becoming what I've termed as hybrid-vegetarian. Not that I have any ethical dilemma with eating meat; but, I am also conscientious of the negative consequences of the consumption of meat, the treatment of the animals it comes from, and the subsequent environmental effects. I've found myself an advocate for part-time vegetarianism. A person whom attempts to eat 50% less meat has committed themselves to a healthier lifestyle not only for themselves but for the world as well. Vegetarians be proud, but you're still not going to pry the occasional chili-cheese burger from my hands. The difference now is when I make my burger it's from 94/6 lean low fat beef. Switching your meat purchases to the lowest fat available has one of the most significant affects on your fat intake.

Various other meats like ground chicken and ground turkey are available. Carefully examine the fat content as often certain blends are fattier than their beef counterparts.

When buying chicken, buy only lean skinless breast meat, and for recipes which require steak, using a London broil or top round cut is the only way to go.

Lean turkey can also be purchased, as can white fish. Examine the label to be sure the meat you put in your meal is the healthiest choice you can make.

Some Typical Lean Meats (4oz)

Meat	Fat	Calories
Top Round	6.3g	210
Pork Tenderloin	4.9g	188
Top Sirloin	8.2g	260
Ham Steak	9.0g	150
White Ground Turkey	3.5g	130
94/6 Ground Beef	4.5g	140
93/7 Ground Beef	8.0g	170
Turkey Sausage	4.5g	140
Turkey Bacon	3.0g	50
Center Cut Bacon	8.0g	100

Dairy:
Personally, I couldn't live without cheese. There are a lot of low-fat and light cheeses available, but my favorite and the one I recommend is Cabot 75 Vermont cheese. In my opinion Cabot's tastes more like the full-fat version, and is available at most major food chains plus it melts like the fattier traditional cheeses. It's well worth the price with the savings of fat which is 2.5g of fat per serving. Be careful as there is a Cabot 50, and they do make full fat cheeses.

Another great brand is Borden's fat-free slices for sandwiches. If neither of these are available in your area, then it's likely other brands are.

Read the packages, and be sure to try multiple brands to find the texture, taste and fat content you like.

An obvious mention is skim fat-free milk, fat-free cottage cheese, and fat-free sour cream as well; in addition to, fat free creamers available for your coffee and fat-free cream cheese.

Fat Cheese Chart

	Fat Grams 1 ounce	Calories 1 ounce
Skim Mozzarella	4.5	70
Whole Mozzarella	6.0	80
American	8.0	100
Brie	8.0	100
Monterey Jack	8.0	100
Swiss	8.0	100
Parmesan	8.5	130
Cream Cheese	10	100
Gruyère	9.2	117
Light Velveeta	3.0	62
Cabot 75	2.5	60

Secondary Meats: Bacon, and Sausage:

Turkey bacon is by far one of the best ways of cutting huge amounts of fat out of your diet. Even different brands of turkey bacon can have drastically different fat grams, so read the label and educate yourself. I generally prefer *Butterball* brand as it's only 1.5 grams of fat.

There is a major difference in taste between traditional bacon, and turkey bacon. As an alternative, *center-cut bacon* is the perfect full taste replacement. It's half the fat of normal bacon but tastes just the same.

Another breakfast food, sausage is commonly available as a turkey sausage with a much reduced fat content. It's fairly common in major hypermarkets, but if you can't find it, you can always make your own using lean ground turkey or pork and seasoning it.

Eggs:
Eggs, I've found are one of the easiest replacements. With egg substitute products so cheap, containing zero grams of fat, and tasting just like real eggs- it's truly a no-brainer.

There was a bit of a negative ad campaign by egg producers back in the 1980s leaving many to ponder what exactly is in egg substitute, but in general, it's nothing more than egg-whites. While a traditional egg doesn't kill you from time to time, (it is after all a high protein food) the savings in fat will make you reach for the egg substitute every time.

Potatoes, Chips, Crisps, Frites and Fries:
So many of the things we eat aren't inherently bad, it's the fact that they're prepared in a manner that is unhealthy that lends itself to our large waistlines. There are some great alternatives like baked chips, and even fat-free ones. They're healthier and taste just as good. Next time you make French fries, simply bake them and you'll never miss the deep-fried oils.

Desserts:
Contrary to popular belief, fat-free baking isn't all that difficult. In this book we well demonstrate several techniques from the traditional dieter's angel food cake for strawberry shortcake, to fudge brownies, and banana nutter bread.

Fast Food:
Find a replacement for your fast-food habits. Replacing
that fast-food breakfast that you argue "is quick and all I
have time for", for one of the healthier options at your
grocer and can be prepared in just seconds in a microwave
can make a huge difference in the amount of fat you take
in for breakfast.

Having options available before you get in the car
hungry and drive by your favorite fast-food addiction can
make a huge difference in your success.

But let's get real, you're going to eat fast food from
time to time. You can, however make smart decisions
while on that road trip, or that occasional shopping trip
with the girls or guys. What I encourage you to do, is do
what I did. Research all the restaurants you'd normally eat
at. Most of them have websites and they're required by law
to have nutrition information available for the consumer.

Sometimes that chicken sandwich you think is
healthy, really isn't. Occasionally you'll even discover that
cheeseburger you're craving is oddly less fat than the
chicken sandwich. With a bit of preparation and self-
education you'll learn very quickly what foods are bad,
and what's horribly bad.

A few Breakfast Fast Food Examples:

Menu Item	Fat
McDonald's Egg McMuffin	12g
McDonald's Hotcakes	9g
McDonald's Sausage Burrito	16g
McDonald's Scrambled Eggs (2)	11g
Jack in The Box Breakfast Jack	12g
Dunkin Doughnuts Whole Grain Bread Sandwich	6g
Burger King Ham Omelet Sandwich	13g
Hardee's Cinnamon Raisin Biscuit	12g

I mentioned both the Egg McMuffin, and the flat bread sandwich in the following subsequent review I wrote for publication:

Dunkin Doughnuts
August, 2008

Dunkin Doughnuts is making a comeback. They're secretly, and quite honestly doing good job at it re-inventing their product in comparison to the competition.

What is it that Dunkin Doughnuts is doing that's causing such a stir that people are clamoring to the place and breaking down the door? Health. That's right. When stock of Krispy Kreme declined in response to the Atkins craze, and healthy lifestyles, Dunkin Doughnuts re-invented themselves as a healthy coffee bar, that provides a niche market to those looking for a healthy choice in the morning routine.

In addition they have great coffee, and their always popular line of doughnuts.

Up till now the only healthy fast food breakfast item that I was aware of was McDonald's original egg McMuffin. (The Canadian bacon one, not the sausage one.) It's not a spectacular breakfast, nor is it breaking any world record for healthiness but at 12g of fat it sets itself apart from the competition which are commonly between 25-50g of fat, and that's not including the hash browns. While the 12g seems a lot, considering most of it comes from a protein source like the eggs and Canadian bacon it's really a lot better than anything out there.... and that's the point. I wish there was more.

That's where Dunkin Doughnuts comes in with their whole grain, flat bread, egg white breakfast sandwich. That's right, you read that right. Whole grain, egg whites, from a doughnut company. A responsible business plan from the least likely of sources. Other fast foods should take a look at what they're doing. It's clear there's a market for it, but up till now, no one else was offering it.

Today I tried a egg white and sausage flat bread sandwich. I asked for a veggie, but got this.... That's OK. It's still amazing. Only 6g of fat (half of the Egg McMuffin if you're keeping score), and it's the size of a slice of pizza. It tastes amazing, fulfilling, and best of all absolutely no guilt afterwards.

The biggest trouble is steering clear of the
doughnuts while you're in there. The flat
bread was crunchy, and the egg and meat
mixture was like a light fluffy omelet. I
highly recommend this sandwich so you too
can run on the healthiest fast food breakfast
out there.

Lunch and Dinner Fast Food Examples:

Menu	Fat
Blimpie's Chicken Teriyaki, no cheese	6g
Quizno's Black Angus Sub, no cheese	8.5g
Chick-fil-A's Char-grilled Chicken Sandwich	3g
Burger King Whopper JR (no mayo or cheese)	12g
Burger King Veggie Burger (no cheese or mayo)	8g
McDonald's BBQ Snack Wrap	9g
McDonald's Grilled Chicken BLT	12g
Moe's Triple Lindy (no cheese, sour cream, beans)	14g
Jack in the Box (1) Taco	8.5g
Jack in the Box Side Salad	3g
Sonic Corn Dog	11g
Domino's Philly Steak Pizza (large)	8g per slice
In-n-Out Hamburger with mustard, no spread	10g
Wendy's Small Chili	6g
Wendy's Ultimate Grilled Chicken Sandwich	7g
Taco Bell's Soft Taco	9g
Taco Bell's Fresco Menu	10g or less

Taco Bell
July, 2008

A major misconception is that there is a defined, set Fresco menu at Taco Bell, when in actuality there isn't. As long as you add the word "Fresco" to anything on their menu, they prepare it a special way which is 25% less fat. So exactly what is the "Fresco" getting you? Removal of cheese and sauce! Surprisingly it doesn't lead to the removal of beans, which is likely responsible for another 25% of the fat. So technically saying "Fresco minus beans" will probably be even better.

Yes that's right. Low fat tacos, Mexican pizzas, etcetera and so on. How does this work out on a menu which is already fat wise one of the healthier fast foods out there? Well you can get a Rancher Chicken Soft Taco for 4 grams of fat or a steak taco for 4.5 grams of fat. That's awesome. No, really.

I spent a few minutes last night going through some of the other major fast food companies (McDonald's, Burger King and Wendy's) and the only things that came close were the grilled chicken sandwiches at generally 3 to 4 times the amount of fat, and their salads.

I hope this wakes fast food companies up. You can offer low-fat versions of great tasting food and it's very alluring to many of us.

For instance, how about a low-fat cheeseburger? Simple as 94/6 beef at 4.5 grams of fat, some fat free cheese (or even 2%), add the condiments minus the mayo, and you've got a healthy cheeseburger alternative that tastes great and under 6-7 grams of fat on a whole wheat bun. So why don't they do it?

Mexican food in general when you're in a pinch is generally a responsible decision. It's not like it's a miracle of the fast food industry, but typically it's low in carbohydrates, (no bun, only a thin tortilla, etc.) high in protein, and loaded with vegetables. (Well, at least for some of us.)

We've got a great restaurant in my area called Moe's Southwest Grill. They're a nationwide chain so you may want to check if there is one in your area. The restaurant is based around the simple idea of fresh, *healthy* Mexican food, though you do have to watch as several things on their menu which can be high in fat. For example you can purchase a burrito they call the *Triple Lindy* which if ordered without beans, sour-cream, or cheese comes to only 14 grams of fat. You're still getting a huge steak burrito with rice, pico de gallo, and any vegetable you desire! If you're a hybrid or going full vegetarian they offer tofu, or ½ tofu and ½ meat burritos. I must admit on occasion I'll treat myself to the cheese and sour-cream which comes in at 29 grams of fat.... but let's think about that for a moment. A Big Mac is also 29 grams of fat and it's considerably less food than the burrito. Also, let us consider where the fat is coming from.

Is it coming from the cheese, lean meat, or sour cream as it is in the burritos case or from a huge greasy ground beef patty which was purchased from the lowest bidder, whom mixed the meat with extra animal fat in a manufacturing plant to subsidize the cost of your McSandwich, shipped to a restaurant in a semi-truck, then subsequently drowned in one of the highest fat content "special sauces" in the industry and served to you in your car through a window in the side of the building as you inhale car exhaust from the idling cars in front of you. I think the cheese might be the healthiest part. "I'd like one Big Mac minus the smog please." Remember, I can always order my burrito in a lower fat option (without sour cream and cheese) and still have a huge burrito with half the fat... Try ordering a Big Mac without the meat, or a Big Mac with out the Mac Sauce, it won't quite taste the same.

Subway:
We all know by watching Subway's Jared that Subway is healthy. Though I think I'd murder someone if I ate Subway every meal as Jared did to lose weight, the premise of their core business model is definitely true and can be an option. But remember most all the sandwiches they claim are low fat are minus the cheese, subtract the mayonnaise, and without the additional Oil. I'll typically order my Subway sandwiches with just salt, pepper and vinegar and disregard the mayo and oil. I've never noticed a difference.

Domino's:
Domino's thin crust pizza is always a healthy option. They also allow you to denote "light on cheese" which reduces your calories and as long as you steer away from the meats, it's one of the healthier fast foods out there.

Others:

It's important to mention these are but a few of the smarter
options out there. Again, take a look before you go to eat,
or order up and you can generally always find a smarter
decision which is just as satisfying as your previous habit.

It's the American Way

So why does fast food, or even food in general seem so bad for us. As I will demonstrate in this book it's very possible to make low-fat great tasting food at home as savory as the unhealthy versions we're accustomed to. America's obsession with having food- now, cheap, and loaded with calories seems to be the major reason for obesity in the country. It's a matter of the fact that we've stopped paying attention to what we put into our bodies. A couple decades ago if you wanted to eat, you'd probably have to cook at least some of it. Today, we think of most foods as coming already partially prepared. Some of us rarely even use our kitchens anymore other than to store soft-drinks and prepackaged foods.

While both the British and Americans are suffering from an obesity epidemic; metropolitan areas of Britain such as London tend to have healthier foods, and less overweight citizens.

I had the recent opportunity to visit London, and while I was there I became interested in how most of the fast food served by American franchises in the U.K. were generally lower fat.

I had a Big Mac across from our hotel one day hoping to find it curiously different, but it wasn't. It tasted just like our American Big Mac except for one small difference. It was 5 grams less than the American cousin it descended from. I was shocked.

Domino's offered a similar comparison along with a low-fat cheese option, and lower fat content in general compared to their American counterparts.

Are these U.S. Versions of these companies purposely making us fatter, or do government restrictions (or the lack thereof) affect the ingredients? In the case of the Big Mac, there was no noticeable difference. So I guess the question is if they can make it healthier, why aren't they?

Another important portion of the London lifestyle was the form of transportation that is seemingly lacking in the U.S.- public. I mean, we clearly have various forms of public transportation, but the majority of our population centers have nothing like their *Underground*. Taking *The Tube* (an interconnected highway of rail lines, and multiple, repeating subway trains) to and from work, home or where ever one might need to go, requires a good amount of exercise just getting to and from the stations. Changing lines or even just standing in a full carriage is a far change from sliding into your leather seats of your American made 15 mile per gallon bright yellow Hummer parked in your climate controlled garage, connected to your living room.

Let me clarify that walking and changing lines isn't really all that much of a burden. It's actually nice to stand, walk, and get some fresh air on a rail platform waiting for the next train. You don't have to deal with a single red light, traffic jam, or soccer mom so filled with road rage she's giving you the middle finger in her rear view mirror as her kids cry with their faces pressed to their windows mouthing "HELP ME" to the other motorists! What's even more interesting is the social aspect. You actually talk, and meet people when you're sharing a bench seat with twenty of your closest neighbors. I'm not saying the Brits are big talkers but you're more likely to strike a conversation up on *the Tube* than talking to yourself in your 1979 Pontiac Trans-Am you've nicknamed "the son of Trigger" because you see yourself as a Burt Reynolds rebel-type for refusing the carpool lane and riding *Lone Ranger*, so to speak. Americans never talk to one another anymore. Our television-news reporter's favorite past-time is to catch the pregnant teenage mother in front of the mobile home with a cigarette in her mouth describing her neighbor who went nuts and stuck rat poison in their wife's lasagna: "He seemed nice. He was quiet. Never talked to anyone." We build fences around our yards, gates around our communities, and most of us refuse carpools and public transportation. Then we go to the office in secure buildings with security guards at the door, to hide in our tiny little cubicles at work, and then go home and do it all over again. I used to feel like Bill Murray in *Groundhog Day*. It's a wonder anyone ever meets anyone else other than in business meetings. Which reminds me, I've got to ask my spouse for a raise.

Even in smaller cities in the U.K. like Cardiff, with their compact nature and centralized city structure, the lifestyle there encourages less motor transportation and more walking.

Landing stateside, and coming back home, I found myself putting down the keys at any opportunity I could and relying on the often forgotten marvel of modern transportation: my own two feet. Surprisingly I lost weight, met people, and saved a ton of money on gasoline.

Another piece of the puzzle was a difference in the manner which foods are presented to the public. Nutrition labels appear on the front of many products in the U.K. rather than the back in the U.S. European manufacturers placed the the information that consumers require; to make educated decisions, in a less ignorable more obvious place, rather than the often "out of sight, out of mind" location American products adhere to. In addition; a red light, yellow light, and green light symbol on many products quickly identifies the food as "high fat", "medium fat", or "low fat", simplifying the decision making process, especially when one is in a hurry.

One explanation I learned after becoming intrigued with the comparison of health foods in these two otherwise seemingly similar countries, is the U.K. government's pro-active stance at perpetuating laws to remove harmful trans fats in foods. A similar grassroots effort is underway in the United States, but has been less effective at creating federal legislation to force reluctant food vendors to make the change. In fact on my last trip to Cardiff, I happened to buy a bag of regular crisps, (potato chips) and it was only once I sat down to eat this savory treat that I read on the the label that its manufacturer proudly boasted it had reduced the fat in the product three years in a row. Imagine that, a company making their product better not because they have to, but because it's the right thing to do!

Britain's proactive stance on nutrition extends into their schools as well.

Britain's School Food Trust requires a 14 nutrient based standard for students enrolled in public schools with defined amounts of protein, fats & other nutrients for a properly balanced diet. Initial challenges of instituting such strict requirements were the older students acceptance of the new foods. Primary students whom were not accustomed to the previous foods actually increased by about 2.3% the year following the programs. (Source: BBC News "Meals take-up rises in primaries" 7/10/2009) Meaning more students ate their healthy school lunches than they did the previous unhealthy versions. In nearby Scotland sweets and sodas are banned in all schools. Compared to the square cafeteria style pizza I was fed daily for almost 12 years, the U.K. appears to have decided the best way to tackle obesity is from childhood.

Perhaps there will come a time, even in the U.S. when foods are prepared not because they're the cheapest, or because they will make greater profits for investors; but, because it's healthier and better for us as a society, for our families, our children and most of all, ourselves. I think my *Box Hypothesis* is indicative of something greater. Some internal dichotomy we all have. Some kind of evolutionary left-overs in our genetic code telling us to handle danger (which in this case is food which historically came from animals that we hunted) by using either fight-or-flight. The British, though they suffer with the same issues have chosen to "fight" or confront their problems. Their collective willingness to tackle other issues in a like manner such as public transportation and a national health service has bled over into their nutrition and lifestyle. While as Americans we've chosen the "flight" path. To ignore, to shy away, even to hide in our cars, homes, and cubicles while ridiculing anyone who might suggest that: we, though a great country, should consider *the American way* negotiable when non-Americans succeed and we fail.

Cooking Techniques

Fat-Draining:
One of key elements to cooking low-fat is removing as much of the fat from the meats as possible. The simplest technique for doing so after choosing to purchase low fat meats, is to take your crumbled meats after they're cooked and drain them in a colander. Run hot tap water over top until the water runs clear, rinse the pan, and return the meat to the pan.

Cooking Patties:
The healthiest way to cook hamburger, sausage, turkey or any meat patty is by making the patties thin which reduces calories, fat and cook time. Take two pieces of wax paper and split one pound of ground meat into eight equal balls. Place second sheet of wax paper on top and flatten till the patties are slightly larger then your bun. Carefully remove top sheet of wax paper, sprinkle with salt, and freeze for about 15 minutes. This will make the thinner patties partially solid, and easier to transfer to your pan.

Trim all visible Fat:
 Even though we use only lean meats, it's always important to trim any visible fat. It's often difficult to throw new food away, but it's even more difficult to throw those added pounds away gained by eating it. On the other hand, my dog loves when I butcher the top-round as it always involves a special treat.

Sauté:
Throughout this book, I make several references to sautéing onions, peppers or other vegetables. In general I rarely use anything other than a good non-stick skillet sprayed with non-fat olive oil spray, some salt and pepper and a few minutes of heat.

Substitutions:
This is a huge part of this book. The recipes that you find, try and like in this book are only the beginning. It's about learning how to change your favorite recipe into something healthier that makes this lifestyle a success. Here are a few examples of full fat versions of ingredients, and their replacements:

sour cream	fat free sour cream
cottage cheese	fat free cottage cheese
butter	light margarine / yogurt
eggs	egg substitute
rice	brown rice
bread	whole grain / sour dough
pork sausage	turkey sausage
ground Beef	96/4% lean ground beef
chips	baked chips or fat free chips
vegetable oil	extra virgin olive oil (EVOL)
cheeses	Borden Slices / Cabot 75
bacon	turkey bacon / center cut
ice cream	non-fat ice cream or yogurt
whipped cream	fat-free whipped topping
cream cheese	fat-free cream cheese

Proofing:
There are two proofing methods mentioned in this book for pizza and coca in addition to assumed traditional methods. They can be used interchangeably based on your preference and time available.

One is *delayed fermentation* in which dough is proofed slowly, overnight. This process produces excellent results. It is highly recommended if you are to use white and wheat flour mix.

The quicker alternative, is traditional proofing by using your oven as a commercial proofer.

Especially during the winter, my home is rarely hot enough for counter-top proofing, so I simply preheat my oven to 200F, wait till the light goes out, and then shut off the oven. Then I place my kneaded and mixed dough (in a glass or metal bowl covered in tin foil) into the oven and allow it to rise for 30-45 minutes.

F.E.B.:
When it comes to battering vegetables and meats the easiest way to remember how to batter foods is F.E.B., as in **F**lour, **E**gg, **B**readcrumbs, in that order. Cornflakes make great breadcrumbs if you crush them in a plastic bag.

Cooking a Steak:
Inevitably at some point or another the craving hits to have a steak. When it does, I don't hesitate. Protein in the presence of fat is better than eating something with no dietary value. The late Dr. Robert Atkins proved removing carbohydrates from a diet altered the bodies metabolism in a way which causes the human body to be starved of glucose as energy and thus burn its stored fat in place of the carbohydrates. Subsequent methodologies suggest a pattern of two days of protein followed by a third day of normal carbohydrate / protein mix diet; "resets" the metabolism.

If you fancy to take a stab at it... set your stove-top to medium high and get an approximately 1" thick cut of steak. Preheat the pan, sprayed with non-stick cooking spray and then place your steak and begin timing. Don't flip, don't smash, just cook, season, and time:

Rare	1 minute each side
Medium-Rare	2 minutes each side
Medium	3 minutes each side
Medium-Well	4 minutes each side
Well Done	5 minutes each side

Then remove your steak from heat and allow it to rest at room temperature for at least half of its cook time. It will continue to cook from residual heat.

Oven Temperatures:
I felt it was worth mentioning that no single oven or stove-top bakes or cooks the same, and to use cooking times and temperatures from this and other books as a suggestive reference guide only.

NOSH!
THE INTERNATIONAL DIET COOKBOOK
A PRIMER IN COOKING

Catalina Spice Mix

Named after Catalina Hernandez, Shannon's grandmother. Catalina traveled from Mexico to the United States and with it her culture of authentic Mexican cooking to pass on to her children and grandchildren.

This seasoning developed in her honor is a mix of seasonings which is a core to so many Mexican recipes, and is indispensably convenient when prepared in advance.

This makes enough to store, and season about 20 future dishes. Use an old spice jar and re-label.

Ingredients:

- 2 tablespoons of chili powder
- 2 tablespoons of paprika
- 1 tablespoon of onion powder
- 1 tablespoon garlic powder
- 1 tablespoon of salt
- 1 tablespoon of dried cilantro seasoning flakes

- 2 teaspoons of ground cumin
- 1 teaspoon of black pepper
- 1 teaspoon of cayenne pepper
- 1 teaspoon of crushed red pepper flakes
- 1 tablespoon of dried oregano

Method:

1. Mix all.

2. Store in plastic container, or old re-labeled spice bottle for when needed.

Steakhouse Seasoning

It's dinner time. I like my steak medium-rare, covered in A-1 with some huge well cooked mushrooms on the side. Slap some fat-free or light Caesar dressing on some lettuce with some low-fat Parmesan cheese, and I'm happy. It's sort of like those fancy steak restaurants without the snooty tip mongering waitresses, the vibrating pagers and the two hour wait.

Ingredients:

- 1 teaspoon salt
- 1 teaspoon onion powder
- 1 teaspoon of garlic powder
- ½ teaspoon of black peppercorn ground fresh
- ½ teaspoon crushed red pepper flakes
- ½ teaspoon paprika

Method:

1. Mix together with raw steak and cook. Seasons up to approximately two pounds of top round.

Mexican Rice

It's one thing to toss a lot of oil or butter in your rice. It's an entire thing all together to make a rice that goes great with vegetarian dishes, as well as those in the traditional sense without the fat. This recipe has no oil, no butter, tastes great and is perfect to fill tacos, burritos, or enchiladas. It's not a *Spanish rice* in the traditional sense, since it includes no tomato paste or sauce, but uses several flavors to accent your main dish. It's the perfect combination of flavors and colors to accent great Mexican food.

QUICK FACTS ON RICE:

- The word *rice* literally means "food" or "meal" in Mandarin and Japanese. It symbolizes luck, life, wealth and fertility and is traditionally used in ceremonial rituals such as marriage.

- In Asian cultures; songs, poems, and festivals celebrate with rice.

- Rice which is technically apart of the grass family, is actually the seed of the rice plant.

Mexican Rice

Ingredients:

- 2 cups of rice
- 32 oz chicken broth
- juice from ½ a lime.
- 2 teaspoons "Catalina spice mix" (page: 47)
- chopped "fresh" cilantro leaves.
- 2 cloves of chopped garlic

Method:

1. Place all ingredients minus the cilantro in a medium sized pan and bring to a boil.
2. Reduce heat to medium-low, cover and cook untouched for 18 minutes. (36 for brown.)

2. Once cooked, fluff, and stir in fresh cilantro.

Alternate Version:

If you're vegetarian (or prefer an alternate version), you can always replace the broth with four cups of water and two large Knorr vegetable bouillon cubes.

Mexican Restaurant Style Salsa

So here's the dilemma. You're craving Mexican food, but don't want to spend the money on going out to the local Mexican restaurant only to find you've blown your diet as well as your checking account balance. Of course, you'd make it at home, but it's that restaurant salsa you want that you just can't seem to find at your grocer that is stopping you. Why does the taqueria (taco stand) taste so much better?

Lets first sort out exactly what salsa is. Translated from Spanish, it basically means sauce. More precisely it doesn't involve cowboys nor a "New York City" tag line. Real salsa is either red or green. Red salsa is your normal variety of tomato based taco sauce. Green is called *salsa verde*. There is also something called *pico de gallo* which is a combination of chopped tomatoes, onions, cilantro and seasonings.

So what is real salsa? Real Mexican salsa is so simple, so easy, it's going to blow your mind when I tell you how easy it is to make. But unless, you grew up in Tijuana, or have a Hispanic friend willing to divulge the secrets of true Mexican cuisine, then you wouldn't know how to make it.

Not to overstate the obvious, but salsa goes great on eggs, omelets, even a hamburger. You can dip chips, bread, tortillas or even rice cakes. It's one of the most understated condiments out there, and now you can have it anytime you like as a low-fat, zesty treat.

Mexican Restaurant Style Salsa

Traditional Mild:

The benefits to making this mild salsa is that it's quickly made without cooking, and appeals to almost everyone's palate. It's the ultimate five ingredient salsa that can be made in under five minutes.

Most taquerias and restaurants will simply pour everything into a huge blender, turn it on and serve it in a glass flask.

Ingredients:
- 1- 28oz can of crushed tomatoes
- ½ teaspoon of salt
- ½ teaspoon of garlic powder
- 3 (approx.) tablespoons of pickled jalapeño rings (and juice)
  (add more to increase heat)
- 10 or more leaves of fresh cilantro

Method:
1. Pour all ingredients into blender or food processor.

2. Blend well, and taste, adjusting flavors as needed.

   *** Be aware that hotness does increase with time.*

Mexican Restaurant Style Salsa

A Modern Caliente (HOT):

It's generally not on the menu but almost every Mexican restaurant has a 'hot' blend of their salsa if you ask. Next time you're out ask for some "salsa caliente", because if you're like me you'll love it hot!

Ingredients:
- 1 six ounce can tomato paste
- 1 sugar substitute packet
- 3 tablespoons of minced jalapeño slices and their juice
- 1 tablespoon of dried onion flakes
- 2 teaspoons salt
- ½ teaspoon of garlic powder
- finely diced fresh cilantro
- 3 cups water
- 3 tablespoons vinegar
- 1 tablespoon of chili powder
- 2 teaspoons of Tabasco brand sauce
- 2 teaspoons cornstarch
- 1 teaspoon cayenne pepper
- 2 teaspoons of *Catalina Spice Mix*
- 1 teaspoon lemon juice

Method:
1. Take jalapeños and blend in food processor to mince.
2. In a small saucepan, add jalapeños, water, tomato paste and all ingredients **minus the cilantro.**
3. Whisk, and stir as you bring mixture to a boil.
4. Simmer for one minute, stirring periodically, remove from heat and allow to cool for about 5 minutes.
5. Add cilantro, stir. Transfer to locking lid plastic bowl, seal and place in refrigerator until chilled.

Pico De Gallo

Pico de gallo is the third type of salsa which comically translates to "beak of rooster". It's the Mexico's take on the fruit salad, and gains its name from the style in which you dig it out of a bowl with a chip. (Similar to a chicken pecking at its food.)

Instead of unhealthy snacks, I can make a bowl of this with some baked low fat chips and enjoy my favorite movie night without guilt.

The irony of Pico De Gallo is, it's generally better chilled and served the next day; however, good luck on not eating the whole bowl during your next Audrey Hepburn movie night and having it last that long.

Ingredients:

- 5 chopped tomatoes
- chopped cilantro
- ¼ chopped white onion
- ¼ chopped red onion
- 2 teaspoons of *Catalina Spice Mix*
- 1 teaspoon of chopped pickled jalapeños
- juice of ½ a lime
- 3-5 drops of Tabasco brand hot sauce.

Method:

1. Mix all ingredients in bowl.
2. Chill for 30 minutes.

3. Enjoy.

Homemade Flour Tortillas

I know many people today both foreign nationals, and
Americans buy their tortillas pre-made. In certain urban
areas, tortilla stands (businesses which produce tortillas
like bakeries make breads) will even make them for you
fresh. While certainly there are easier methods, having a
real home made tortilla that has been hand pressed, warm,
and fresh off the iron skillet is not only a talent you'll
cherish, but a flavorful treat you'll impress the family and
the taste buds with. It takes some effort to get them right,
but they're definitely worth the effort if you get the
technique right.

Ingredients:

- 2 cups flour
- 2 teaspoons baking powder
- ¾ cup of water + 2 tablespoons of water
- ½ teaspoon of salt
- fat-free cooking spray.

Method:

1. Mix dry ingredients in bowl.
2. Add wet ingredients and mix.
3. Knead dough till all is combined.
4. Make balls from dough.
5. Press in tortilla press or by hand.
6. On cast-iron skillet sprayed with fat-free spray. Fry tortilla on both sides.

Pizza Dough (White Pizza)

Pizza is a curious creature. It is without a doubt one of the last true arts in food. Like a magician, most people don't understand the science, or art of creating a good pizzeria style pizza at home. It's actually not all that difficult, it just takes several factors to happen in the right sequence in order for the dough to come out just right. A method called delayed fermentation is similar to what large pizza chains use, and with proper patience the beginner pizza maker can succeed at making great tasting pizza dough at home. This is the preferred method if you choose to use wheat-mix flours. If you need a quicker method, an alternative technique is mentioned later in this book to make Cuban cocas and my Pissaladière. Feel free to use them interchangeably to proof your dough.

White pizza or pizza bianca is a type of pizza which uses no tomato sauce as in the case of the steak pizza I'll mention later in this book. In Rome, bianca or white pizza is a bread drizzled with olive oil. Feel free to experiment using anything, but my favorite way is to top it with bocconcini balls, baby plum tomatoes, and fresh spices.

PIZZA QUICK FACTS:

- 17% of all restaurants are pizzerias
- 1/3 of all pizzas ordered are pepperoni
- Brazilian pizza includes peas.
- Pizza was originally spelled pitsa.
- Pizza in India, includes pickled ginger and tofu.

Pizza Dough (White Pizza)

Ingredients: (for 1 large pizza)

- 2.5 cups of bread flour
- 1 cup + 1 tablespoon of cold water
- 1 packet of rapid rise yeast (2¼ teaspoons)
- ½ teaspoon of salt
- 1 teaspoon sugar
- non-fat spray
- zipper bags

Method:

1. In large bowl add flour, salt, sugar, and dry-yeast. Mix with fork. Add water, and create ball of dough by mixing ingredients.
2. Knead dough for several minutes.
3. Spray a large (freezer style) zippered plastic bag with non-fat cooking spray, and place dough ball in bag. Close bag, and place in refrigerator over-night furthest from air vent. (typically in the bottom)
4. Remove dough from refrigerator and place in room-temperature environment in a bowl approximately 1 hour prior to baking.
5. Preheat oven to 450° F.
6. Take a large pizza sheet and coat with corn meal (or non stick spray) and spread dough over top, top with favorite veggies, marinara, and low-fat cheese.
7. Bake for approximately 10 minutes on middle rack then an additional 2 minutes on the bottom rack.

Try seasoning your crust:

Take some melted low fat butter or margarine, a bit of garlic powder, and brush it on to the crust after you bake it. Then sprinkle some low fat Parmesan cheese!

Italian Marinara

A quick and basic recipe for Italian Marinara. Top pizzas, sandwiches, or keep some around just for dipping sauce.

Feel free to make it your own by sweating some onions, or adding a cup of wine into the mix. While leaving out the olive oil almost feels like a sin, this flavor filled Italian gravy is a much healthier rendition.

If you're a carnivore and love meat in your spaghetti try using a chopped up low-fat turkey pepperoni in your marinara. It's a distinct familiar flavor that gives your pasta a truly eclectic taste.

Need a stunning pasta dish? Try comrade's Russian pasta mentioned later in this book. You won't be disappointed.

Ingredients:

- 28 oz can of crushed tomatoes
- 28 oz can of drained diced tomatoes
- 6 cloves garlic (minced)
- 3 sugar substitute packets
- ¾ teaspoon of lemon juice
- ¾ teaspoon of salt
- ¾ teaspoon of oregano
- ¾ teaspoon of onion powder
- ¼ heaping teaspoon of basil
- ¼ heaping teaspoon of thyme
- ¼ heaping teaspoon crushed red pepper
- ¼ heaping teaspoon of black pepper

Method:

1. Mix all ingredients in sauce pan and bring to boil.
2. Simmer for 15 minutes.

Non-Fat Buttermilk Biscuits (6 count)

I'm going to be honest. There's nothing like a buttermilk biscuit cooked with a bucket of shortening pressed into the dough, smothered in butter, and baked in a fashion it should be technically considered deep-frying. This isn't a recipe for that. It is however a great tasting replacement, that given your extended life expectancy by switching to these, will ensure you'll never miss the artery clogging version. Besides, who knew you could make fat free biscuits that tasted "oh, so good?"

Ingredients:

- 2¼ cups flour (plus additional for dusting)
- 1¼ cups non-fat buttermilk
- 1 tablespoon baking powder
- 1 tablespoon sugar
- 1 teaspoon salt
- ½ teaspoon baking soda
- 1 tablespoon of Butter Buds

Method:

1. Preheat oven to 450 F.
2. Mix salt, sugar, flour, and baking powder, baking soda, and Butter Buds in a bowl.
3. Stir buttermilk.
4. Add flour to adjust consistency.
5. Move dough to floured cutting board and press flat to ½ inch thick.
6. Cut with biscuit cutter 6 biscuits.
7. Bake for approximately 8 minutes.
8. Glaze with 1 tablespoon of melted low-fat butter or margarine. (optional)

Taco & Burrito Seasoning (for 1 pound of meat)

This recipe almost didn't make it in the book. I've wanted for so long to create a unique, and flavorful taco and burrito seasoning to replace the store bought mixes, but never had too much inspiration till one day I came up with the idea to put a small amount of Tabasco sauce in the seasoning mix.

I kind of like it as it mixes the best of some many different flavors but inherently is still a simplified, easy taco seasoning mix which turns a pound of ground beef into a quick and tasty dinner.

Ingredients:
- ¾ cup of water
- 2.5 teaspoons chili powder
- 1.5 teaspoons of onion powder
- 1 teaspoon of minced dried onion
- 1 teaspoon of salt
- 1 teaspoon of paprika
- 1 teaspoon of flour
- ½ teaspoon garlic powder
- ¼ teaspoon of crushed red pepper flakes
- 1 teaspoon of Tabasco brand hot-sauce
- ¼ teaspoon of cayenne (optional for hot)

Method:
1. Cook thoroughly your meat. If using ground beef- drain, and rinse in colander to reduce fat.
2. Return to pan and add all ingredients.
3. Simmer on medium-low heat for approximately 10 minutes.

Fast Food Style Baked French Fries / Frites / Chips

The world loves French fries. In Belgium where they were invented they call them *frites* and are served with a Dutch *fritessaus*- a mayonnaise like cream sauce. In the U.K. they call them *chips* and are commonly served with malt vinegar and fish; thus the dish: *fish and chips*.

The trick to fast food style French fries is the par-cooking process of the potatoes done at restaurants by double frying. This healthier version saves a ton of fat and calories by removing the moisture by microwave blanching the fries instead. The salt then pulls more moisture out of the potato right before you bake it in a very, very small amount of olive oil. Bon appétit!

Ingredients:
- 3 potatoes (average to small)
- 2 teaspoons of extra virgin olive oil
- ¾ teaspoon of salt
- ¼ teaspoon of all-season salt
- ¼ teaspoon paprika
- ½ teaspoon garlic powder
- pinch of cayenne
- pinch of pepper

Method:
1. Press potatoes using potato press.
2. Place fries on a plate so that they don't touch and microwave for 4-5 minutes.
3. Sprinkle with salt and allow to cool for 5 minutes.
4. In a bowl mix cayenne, paprika, pepper, all-season salt, garlic, and oil.
5. Add fries, and mix with tongs.
6. Place on baking sheet and salt.
7. Bake in preheated oven at 425° F for 8 minutes, turn over and bake for an additional 8 minutes.

Liv's Chili

Chili. It's hands down probably the most important thing you should know how to make. It goes on practically everything, it will warm you when you're cold, it goes great with beer, and I've yet to hear of anyone, anywhere who doesn't love chili.

I've had chili from Cincinnati, Los Angeles, New York, Texas, London and everywhere in between. I've been to Tommy's, Pink's, Tony Packos, and Gold Star. I've definitely tried my share of chili. Chili is a passion of mine. I truly believe these two chili recipes combine the best of the best for a new low-fat chili that rivals the world's best. I'm that proud of it.

Let me explain things. In the world of chili there are two types. *Condiment* chili, and *meal* chili. (Also known as chuck-wagon chili.) Condiment chili generally gets served on burgers, hot-dogs, and French fries; whereas *meal* chili is generally the main dish served in a bowl or served with rice and beans. Here's a recipe for both of my guiltless low-fat recipes.

Chili Quick Facts:

- Chili in its modern incarnation is actually a Texas invention of a traditional Mexican mole- a cinnamon or chocolate meat dish which has descended and evolved from ancient Aztec and Mayan cooks.

- New York City consumes more chili than the entire state of Texas.

- A popular Texas comfort food includes chili, cheese and Fritos.

Liv's Chili

The following two chili recipes are both a medium heat recipe with moderate thickness. Typical to chili, one can make it hotter by adding additional cayenne pepper or thicker by adding more flour.

For Condiment Chili:

Ingredients:
- 1 pound of 96/4 % lean ground beef
- ½ cup of beef broth (low-sodium) (8 ounces)
- ½ cup of water
- ½ fresh diced onion
- 1 tablespoon + 1½ teaspoon of chili powder
- 2 teaspoons white vinegar
- 1 teaspoons salt
- 1 packet of sugar substitute.
- ½ teaspoon paprika
- ½ teaspoon of cumin
- ½ teaspoon garlic powder
- ½ teaspoon dried onion flakes
- ¼ teaspoon of onion powder.
- ¼ teaspoon of cayenne powder (adjust for hotness)
- 1 Tablespoon of all-purpose flour
- pinch of black pepper

Method:

1. Brown ground beef, drain, and rinse in colander.

2. Return to pan and add all ingredients.

3. Simmer on medium-low heat for approximately 10 minutes.

Liv's Chili

For *Meal* Chuckwagon Chili

Ingredients:
- 2 pounds of 96/4 % lean ground beef.
- 2 cups of crushed tomatoes
- 2 cups of water
- 1 tablespoon white vinegar
- ½ fresh diced onion
- 3 tablespoons chili powder
- 2 teaspoons salt
- 1 teaspoon paprika
- 1 teaspoon of cumin
- 1 packet of sugar substitute.
- 1 teaspoon garlic powder
- 1 teaspoon dried onion flakes
- ¼ teaspoon of onion powder.
- ¼ teaspoon of cayenne powder
- 2 Tablespoon of all-purpose flour.
- 1 Tablespoon of corn starch
- pinch black pepper

Method:

1. Brown ground beef, drain, and rinse in colander.

2. Return to pan and add all ingredients.

3. Simmer on medium-low heat for approximately 10 minutes.

NOSH!
THE INTERNATIONAL DIET COOKBOOK
Lunch and Dinner Recipes

Double Chili Cheeseburger

It's worth mentioning a recipe for the sandwich, though the
secret to a chili burger is of course the chili. I've already
given you the chili recipe, now go on and build the perfect
cheeseburger with it.

Traditional chili cheeseburger methodology
includes a basic mustard used almost as a salad dressing.
Placed around your vegetables (dill pickles) to bring out
their taste. The onions you want on the chili so the heat
can permeate into it, and sweat and release their flavoring.

Quite frankly if you're going to make a chili-cheese
burger then you probably should also make chili-cheese
fries. It just sort of goes together. Like chili burgers and
beer. Guinness is preferred, oh and you're going to need
the rest of the afternoon off while you do absolutely
nothing but smile with contentment and Zen

Namaste to the chili burger.

TRY THIS!

Eat like you're in Europe:

Sick and tired of the basic chili cheeseburger? Are
you a thrill seeker ready to try something new? Pubs all
over Europe serve fried eggs on their burgers. Pull out one
small egg, and fry it in a non-stick pan with some fat free
cooking spray. Cook over-hard, and then flavor with a
sprinkle of black pepper. Add this to your chili burger
toppings.

Double Chili Cheeseburger

Double Chili Cheeseburger

Ingredients:
- condiment chili (see recipe on page: 63)
- tomato
- lettuce
- dill pickle
- onion
- 96/4 % ground beef
- ¼ - ½ slice of light Velveeta Cheese (it's the "secret" ingredient)
- mustard
- hamburger buns

Method:

1. Take beef and form 6 patties and place on wax paper on top of cutting board.

2. Freeze for 15 minutes.

3. Chop ingredients add add to hamburger buns.

4. Cook patties over medium-high heat with a pinch of salt.

5. Melt cheese on top.

6. Place on buns, top with chili and enjoy.

New York Style Dirty Water Hot-Dog

New York city has so much to offer in food. With so much culture, the melting pot of America's most famous city is known for one of the simplest of foods: The humble hot-dog. It's a comfort food craved by thousands daily. Cooked in vendor's hot-dog carts and swimming around in a warm pool of water then topped with your choice of toppings it's a legend which has been nicknamed "comfort on a bun."

I figured it's worth mentioning you can in fact get 99% fat free hot dogs. Combined with a low-fat cheese, and my world famous chili... it's a deceptive little piece of the Big Apple without the big city gluttony.

Ingredients:

- sauerkraut
- 99% fat free hot dogs
- Liv's condiment chili (page: 63)
- chopped onion
- mustard
- hot dog buns
- light Velveeta Cheese

Method:

1. Bring sauce pan of water to a boil.
2. Add hot-dogs and reduce to simmer over medium heat.
3. Cook for 5-10 minutes
4. Warm kraut and chili in separate pan.
5. Top hot dogs with all condiments and melt cheese.

Western Bacon Burger

This recipe came from one of our favorite hamburgers which is common in California. It's a delicious cheeseburger topped with smoky barbecue sauce and fried onion rings. I particularly like to add lettuce and tomato to the sandwich, which makes this a mammoth burger.

Oddly enough I'm not one who is usually a huge fan of BBQ sauce, but I love this burger. If you're the same way as me, you might find a new infatuation with barbecue sauce.

Ingredients:

- 96/4 % ground beef
- onion
- egg substitute
- lettuce and tomato
- burger buns
- turkey or center cut bacon
- breadcrumbs
- smoked BBQ sauce
- salt and pepper
- Borden fat-free cheese slices

Method:

1. Form beef patties on cutting board, flattening meat with wax paper. Freeze for about 15 minutes.
2. F.E.B. (flour, eggs and batter) cut onion rings seasoning with a pinch of salt and pepper. Place on non-fat sprayed baking sheet and bake at 425°F.
3.
4. Slice tomato, and chop lettuce. Remove beef patties from freezer and cook with a pinch of salt on stove top. Cook bacon.
5. Assemble burger adding two onion rings, and topping with BBQ sauce.

Sourdough and Monterrey Cheeseburger

This is one of those simple cheeseburger recipes that proves less is sometimes more. Your first inclination is to think "hey it has no toppings!!", but try it. It's just the right flavors, it's simple and it's a burger that doesn't get drowned in condiments.

You may find it interesting that sourdough bread was found to be more healthy than whole-wheat bread because of its leavening and its effects at controlling blood sugar according to the British Journal of Nutrition.

Ingredients:

- 96/4 % ground beef
- light mayonnaise
- tomato
- salt and pepper
- sourdough bread
- Monterrey cheese

Method:

1. Take beef and form 4 patties and place on wax paper on top of a cutting board. Flatten meat till patties are a few inches larger then your buns. Freeze patties for 10-15 minutes.

2. Take bread and slice (if necessary) and toast. Add a thin layer of mayonnaise.
3. Slice tomato.
4. Remove beef patties from freezer and cook with a pinch of salt and pepper on stove top.
5. Assemble burger with 1 hamburger patty, 1 tomato, and 1 slice of Monterrey cheese.

The Winner

Liv's father, proudly displays the winning zucchini at the local competition.

Big Burger

Several fast food restaurants have sandwiches labeled "big". When they first came out they were indeed some of the biggest out there. Today they're dwarfed by the nearly half to one pound burger varieties available at the drive-thru. Today those sandwiches are favored not for their size but their distinct taste.

Ingredients:
- 1 pound 96/4 % ground beef
- Cabot 75 cheese or Borden fat-free slices.
- dill pickles
- shredded lettuce
- hamburger buns

Sauce:
- 1/3 cup finely minced onion
- 1/3 cup finely minced dill pickles
- 1/4 teaspoon of Tabasco or hot sauce
- 1 cup of light mayonnaise

Method:

Sauce:
1. Food process, or hand mince onions and pickles.
2. Strain to remove moisture if necessary.
3. Mix with mayonnaise and Tabasco in bowl.

Burgers:
1. Form 8 patties and place on wax paper on top of a cutting board. Freeze patties for 10-15 minutes.
2. Grill and place two meat patties on a bun.
3. Top with sauce, lettuce, and any additional condiments.

Liv's Lasagna

Here's a perfect example of a family recipe which we made for years in higher caloric version with more fat that can now be enjoyed in the same manner but without the weight gain that follows.

Ingredients:
- 1 pound 94/6 % beef
- ¼ cup egg substitute
- 1 large fat free cottage cheese
- salt & pepper
- 1 package of lasagna noodles
- ¼ pound center cut bacon, cooked and chopped
- 16 oz low fat shredded mozzarella cheese
- Italian marinara (page: 58)
- 1 teaspoon garlic powder

Method:
1. Boil your lasagna noodles per instructions on box.
2. Brown your beef, place in colander and rinse with hot water till fat runs clear.
3. Cook bacon, drain fat, and chop.
4. Dump mozzarella, and cottage cheese, salt, garlic, pepper, and egg substitute into a mixing bowl and stir.
5. Add meats to bowl of cheese and seasonings mix and stir.
6. Add thin layer of sauce to 9x12 lasagna pan then noodles. Layer meat and cheese mixture, adding sauce on top of each layer. Finally top dish with a layer of cheese.
7. Bake on 350° F for 20-40 minutes covered with foil, last 10 min remove to brown cheese.

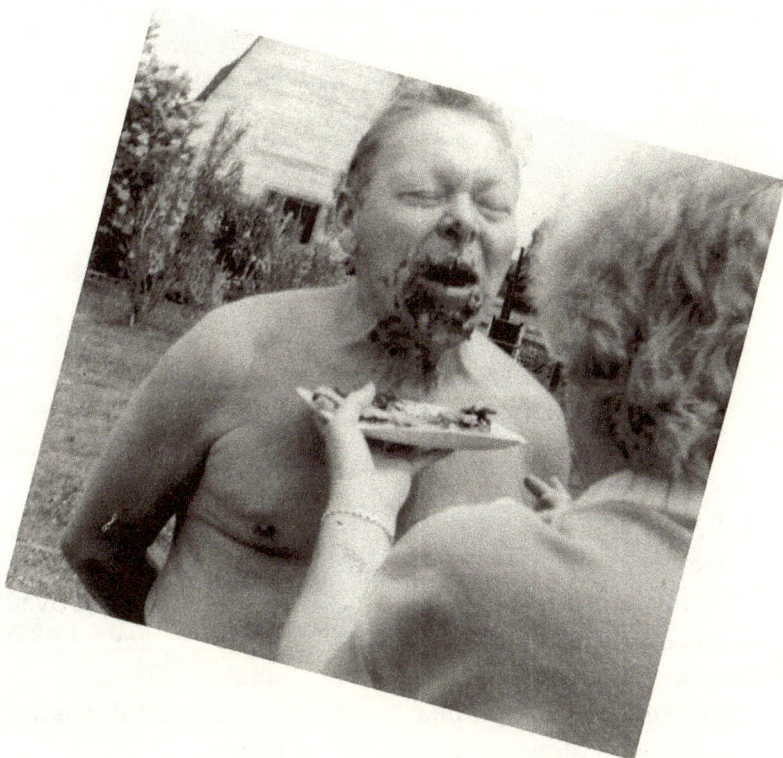

"Fireworks"

July, 4th 1985, Liv's grandfather: Don, in a local pie eating contest.

Chicago Deep Dish Pizza

After I lost about 80 pounds I was getting real close to a goal I had set. Upon hitting that goal I told myself I'd order an authentic Chicago deep dish pizza. Then I got an idea. Why eat all that fat, when I can make one at home, healthier.... and have it taste just as good? So that's exactly what I did.

Ingredients:
- Italian marinara (page: 58)
- pizza dough (page: 57)
- low fat provolone cheese
- low fat-Parmesan cheese
- low fat turkey sausage

Method:

1. Take a 9" Cake pan and place dough in bottom, pressing dough up the side of the pan to create a deep cavity.
2. Take provolone cheese and layer bottom of pie.
3. Brown sausage, drain and rinse. Place on top of cheese.
4. Take large spoonfuls of marinara and top sausage.
5. Bake in preheated oven at 425° F degrees for 18 minutes.
6. Garnish with Parmesan cheese.
7. Remember! Chicago pizza is always respected by using silverware.

Pigs in the blanket

Growing up in Toledo, Ohio- home of the world famous Tony Packo's, I'd be disowned by my hometown if I didn't mention a recipe for their signature dish: Hungarian cabbage rolls. If you're not familiar with the restaurant, you can ask the cast from the hit series M.A.S.H. who scripted in references to the restaurant into almost every episode of the show. Presidential signatures dating back to the restaurant's founding in 1932 line the walls as well most everyone from Hollywood.

Our recipe however, which is so similar.... is a family heirloom. Descended from Europe just as as I'm sure Tony's did. It's that one family recipe that's been passed down from generation to generation and very near and dear to my heart. As a child I'd come home and immediately know what was for dinner the moment I hit the front yard. It put a smile on everyone's face and was a comfort food that reminded us how great life was. Re-inventing it for a whole new generation is an honor, perfecting it was a challenge, but this low-fat version is truly a rite of passage which I can proudly say stays true to its humble beginnings.

Ingredients:
- 1 cup of rice
- 1 pound of lean ground pork
- salt & pepper to taste
- 2 minced garlic cloves
- 1 pound sauerkraut
- 1 large can of tomato sauce
- 1 tablespoon of fat-free sour cream
- 1 large head of green cabbage
- 1 pound of 96/4 % ground beef
- ¼ cup egg substitute
- 2 teaspoons of paprika
- 28oz can of crushed tomatoes
- 2 packets of sugar substitute
- 1 large Knorr vegetable Bouillon cube

Pigs in the blanket

Method:

1. Cook the 1 cup of rice with 16 oz of water (2 cups) and 1 large Knorr vegetable bouillon cube.

2. Place head of cabbage in a large pot and fill with water, bring to boil then remove from heat.

3. Take large mixing bowl and into it place the pork, beef, rice, paprika, garlic, eggs, salt, pepper, and sugar substitute. Mix by hand.

4. Remove and separate full leaves of cabbage off head. Take hand sized lumps of meat mixture and place on a cabbage leaf. Roll cabbage leaves around meat in a burrito fashion tucking both ends in.

5. Pour tomato sauce and crushed tomatoes into large pot(s). Place rolled stuffed cabbage into pot(s). Place lid(s) on pot(s). Set timer for 2 hours and simmer on a low heat adding water as needed to keep rolls covered.

6. At approximately 45 minutes from the end of cooking time stir in 1 tablespoon of sour cream and sauerkraut.

Philly Cheesesteak

A few years back we went to Philadelphia where I got to eat an official Philadelphia cheese steak from both Gino's and Pat's. (The two rival cheesesteak factions in Philadelphia.) I immediately came home and began making them Philly style. Today, I'm still able to enjoy the tastes of the city of brotherly love with my leaner version.

The most important aspect of a Philly cheesesteak is the meat and the whiz. In our case, top-round is a cheap, affordable, and lean meat. It's often on sale for ½ price at my local grocer in a huge three pound package. Ask the butcher to slice it thin and save yourself some work. Whiz is available in *light* which further reduces the fat content of this protein rich sandwich.

Cheesesteak Facts:

- Invented in 1930 when a Philadelphia hot-dog vendor named Pat Olivieri decided to add thin slices of steak on to a hot-dog bun. By 1952 the cheesesteak was officially famous when long time cheesesteak rival Joe Vento of Geno's added Cheese Whiz to the sandwich

- A NY Times article famed the whiz version of the sandwich with the words "the *sine qua non* of cheesesteak connoisseurs", simply translated meaning "without Whiz then nothing."

Philly Cheesesteak

Ingredients:

- sub buns or hoagie rolls
- thin steak slices (top round or London broil)
- 2% light Velveeta cheese sauce
- chopped onion, tomatoes and lettuce
- Steakhouse seasoning (page: 48)

Method:

1. Chop and marinate steak with steakhouse seasonings in a large frying pan.

2. Sear in frying pan over medium-high heat.

3. Add chopped onions, peppers and mushrooms mid-way.

4. Warm bread in oven or on stove-top.

5. Once the meat is cooked shut the burner off, and toss in your tomatoes, and lettuce and mix it all up.

6. Spread 1 tablespoon of 2% cheese sauce on the bun. Place all ingredients in bun.

TRY THIS!

You can also try spicing it up with some green or yellow peppers, black olives or other vegetables!

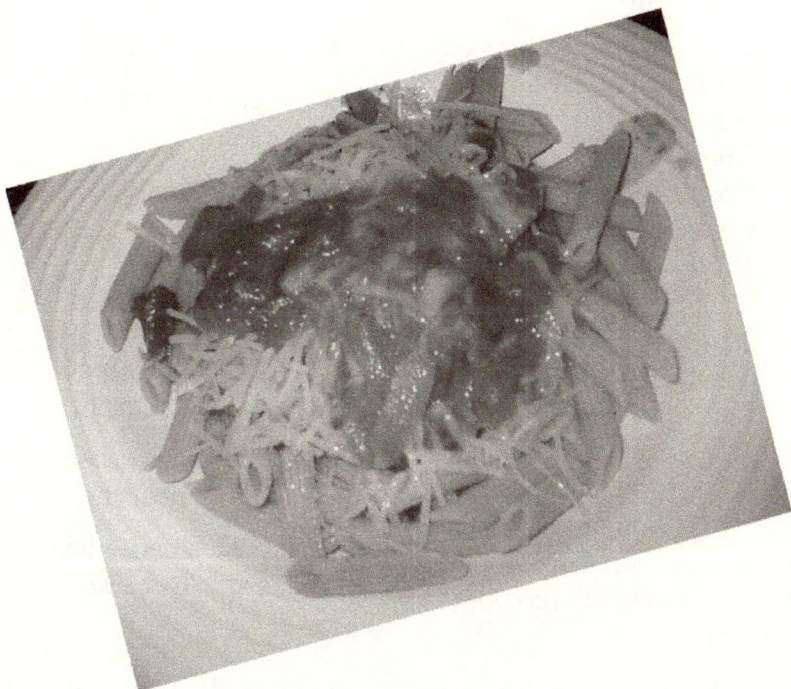

Comrade's Russian Pasta

Comrade's Russian Pasta

Take my marinara sauce add a bit of Vodka, a bit of cream, some sweet onions then call your comrades. They'll thank you for it.

Ingredients:

- 1 Vidalia onion, chopped
- 1 package of fresh whole portobello mushrooms.
- 1 box of wheat penne rigate
- 1 package of fresh sliced white button mushrooms.
- 28 oz can of crushed tomatoes
- 28 oz can of drained diced tomatoes
- 6 cloves garlic (minced)
- 3 sugar substitute packets
- ¾ teaspoon of lemon juice
- ¾ teaspoon of salt
- ¾ teaspoon of oregano
- ¾ teaspoon of onion powder

- ½ cup of Vodka
- ½ cup of fat-free sour cream
- ¼ heaping teaspoon of basil
- ¼ heaping teaspoon of thyme
- ¼ heaping teaspoon crushed red pepper
- ¼ heaping teaspoon of black pepper
- low fat shredded Parmesan cheese

Method:

1. Take a large pot, spray with non-fat cooking spray. Add mushrooms, chopped onion, and garlic into pan, and sweat for 5 minutes.
2. Add crushed and diced tomatoes, garlic, sugar, lemon juice, salt, oregano, onion powder, basic, thyme, red & black peppers. Continue to cook on medium high-heat and stir well.
3. Add sour cream, and vodka, stir well.
4. In a second pot, boil and cook pasta for approximately 9 minutes.
5. Simmer sauce for about 15 minutes.
6. Drain pasta, plate, top with sauce and garnish with low-fat Parmesan cheese.

Sicilian Za Bap

Sicilian food may have some vague familiarity with most American's palettes due to the fact it's a spicier variation of traditional Italian foods.

The food, like the word Sicilian originated from the island of Sicily, Italy whose cuisine, linguistics, and culture became varied as a result of its seclusion from main-land Italy.

Sicilian food is generally fast, great tasting, and relatively cheap.

QUICK FACTS:

- BAP: A 16th century term for any soft bread. Originated when hard breads began to take on qualities of pastries and the process by which yeast produces the bread. Acronym for *Barm and Pastry*

- ZA: A 21st century term for pizza, or pizza related foods.

Sicilian Za Bap

Ingredients:
- bread rolls of your choice.
- Italian marinara (page: 58)
- low-fat light Provolone cheese
- turkey bacon
- light turkey pepperoni
- light mayonnaise
- thin sliced ham
- shredded lettuce
- sliced tomato
- low-fat 1000 island dressing
- yellow sliced banana peppers
- grilled onions

Method:
1. Cook bacon & grill onions.
2. Lightly grill ham and pepperoni on griddle.
3. Warm marinara.
4. Assemble sandwich with mayonnaise, dressing, banana peppers, lettuce, tomatoes, and meats.
5. Place on cooking sheet in preheated oven at 400° F for approximately 6 minutes or until cheese is melted.

Albondigas Meatballs and Rice

Shannon is responsible for this recipe within our family
after altering a traditional Albondigas soup, into a unique
dish of its own.

Ingredients:
- 1 pound 96/4 % lean ground beef
- ¼ teaspoon of garlic powder
- ¼ finely diced onion
- ½ teaspoon ground cumin
- 28 oz can crushed tomatoes

- Mexican rice (page: 50)
- fat-free sour cream

- ¼ cup of saltine crumbs
- chopped fresh cilantro
- ¼ cup egg substitute
- 1/8 cup of water
- 1/8 cup of chopped chipotle peppers in adobe sauce
- baked tortilla chips

Method:
1. Combine and mix beef, cracker crumbs, egg, cilantro, onion, cumin and water.
2. Form into 12-15 meat balls
3. Simmer tomato sauce and peppers, and meatballs for 15-20 minutes stirring occasionally.
4. Serve with rice, garnish with cilantro and sour cream.

The Fisherman

Emil Schnabel, Liv's great grandfather showing off dinner
for the camera.

Chimichangas

Ingredients:

- shredded chicken skinless chicken breasts, or 96/4 % lean ground beef, or top round steak chopped 1/8" thin
- 2 tomatoes chopped
- 1 can chopped green chilies
- 2 tablespoons fresh cilantro
- extra virgin olive oil
- Liv's salsa (page: 52)
- sliced black olives
- ½ pound chopped and cooked center cut bacon pieces.
- ½ onion, diced.
- 2 teaspoons of Catalina spice mix (page: 47)
- flour tortillas
- shredded Cabot 75 cheese
- shredded lettuce

Method:

1. Preheat oven to 350° F
2. Cook meat on stove top, draining and rinsing grease if necessary.
3. Cook, blot and crumble bacon.
4. Saute onion and chiles adding spice mix and cilantro.
5. Mix meat, and bacon with onions and chiles. Add tomatoes, and mix well.
6. Place ½ cup of meat in a tortilla and fold like a burrito.
7. Place seam side down on a non-fat sprayed cooking sheet.
8. Take a very small amount of extra virgin olive oil (½ teaspoon or less) and coat tortilla with fingers.
9. Bake for 7-10 minutes till golden brown.
10. Remove from oven and place on plate.
11. Top with cheese, garnish with tomatoes and olives.

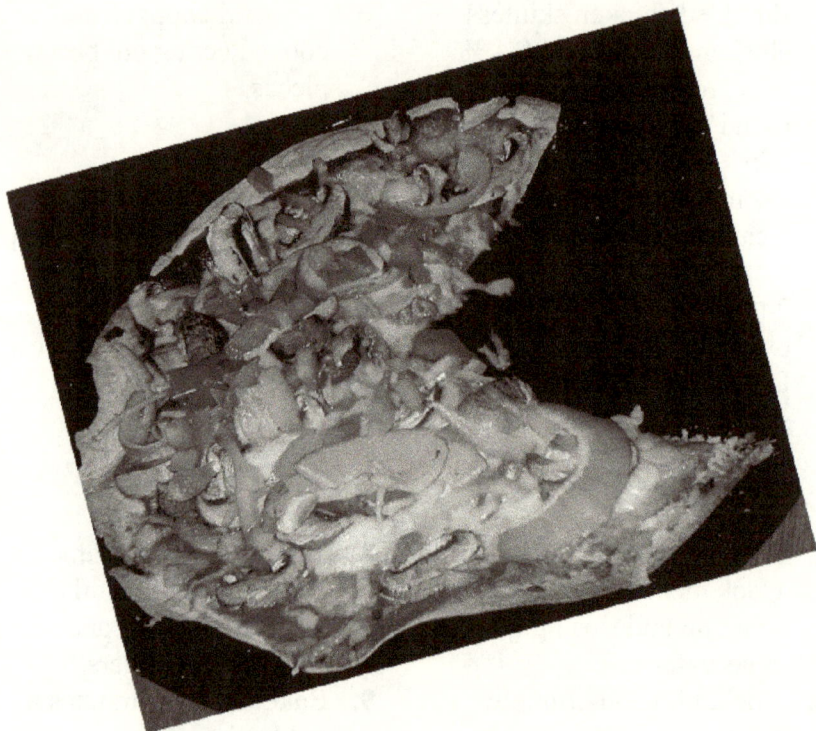

The Healthy Frozen Pizza Alternative

The Healthy Frozen Pizza Alternative

Pizza is one of my favorite foods, and the thought of not being able to eat pizza was a very difficult idea for me to accept. I went in search for healthy options, and not many existed. For a while I used a thin crust wheat pizza which was a great replacement, but then one day on a whim I tried a tortilla. What do you know, it was better.

For 6 grams of fat you can have a delicious veggie pizza. Comprised of 1.5 grams in the tortilla, and 4.5 grams in the light mozzarella cheese. You can lower your fat intake even more by going with Cabot 75 cheddar in lieu of the mozzarella and save an addition 2.5 grams of fat per serving.

Adding additional toppings like black olives, or turkey pepperoni does add additional fat and calories, but if you can't live without them, this is still a much better alternative than your grocer's freezer section offerings.

My spouse makes a low-fat Canadian bacon and pineapple version and loves that the tortillas actually crisp and harden in the oven to form a cracker-like thin crust.

QUICK FACTS:

- The city of Naples, Italy gave birth to the pizza.
- The average Italian consumes 26 gallons of wine a year and half a pound of bread a day.

The Healthy Frozen Pizza Alternative

Ingredients:

- burrito sized tortilla
- Liv's Italian marinara (page: 58)
- baby portobello mushrooms
- red onions
- green peppers
- black olives (optional)
- light mozzarella

Method:

1. Preheat oven to 450° F
2. Place tortilla on pizza sheet.
3. Place empty tortilla in oven for one minute.
4. Remove from oven.
5. Add marinara, and toppings as desired.
6. Re-insert pizza for about 6 minutes.

Chili Rice Con Carne

The night we landed in London we were starved, and
nothing was open. We called room service, and ordered
one of the few things they still had available. They served
us familiar ingredients, but in a very new way. Over rice!
Its closest cousin in the United States would be gumbo,
and is often because of this known as New Orleans Style
Chili; however, chili rice is a popular style of serving chili
in much of Europe, Canada, and other areas of the world.
It's now one of my favorites.

QUICK FACTS:

- According to Mexican lore chili is the food of
  forgiveness and reconciliation.

- Chili con carne which literally translates to "pepper
  with meat" stew.

- Chili enthusiasts believe a true authentic chili con
  carne has no beans. The addition of beans was an
  eastern U.S. addition which has subsequently been
  banned at most official cook offs.

- Many believe that chili con carne became popular
  as a bar food being made of leftovers and given
  away free to cantina goers to increase the amount
  of beer sold.

Chili Rice Con Carne

Ingredients:

- meal chili (page: 64)
- 2 cups rice
- 4 cups water
- 2 garlic cloves, smashed and diced
- 1 teaspoon of paprika
- 1 teaspoon crushed red pepper flakes
- 1 teaspoon onion powder
- shredded Cabot 75 cheese
- chopped onions
- baked tortilla chips
- fat-free sour cream

Method:

1. Cook rice per manufacturer's instructions adding paprika, red pepper, and garlic before cooking.
2. Prepare & cook the chili.
3. Layer chips below a generous proportion of rice and top with chili, shredded cheese and garnish with a tablespoon of non-fat sour cream and chopped onions.

A Better Sloppy Joe

Sloppy Joe's were made famous by the Manwich (slang for *massive sandwich*) brand in 1969. It was American's fascination with the TV dinner and quickly made meals that led to this variation of traditional southern beef barbecue.

I, as many children, grew up with a basic Sloppy Joe on a boring bun. It was adequate then, but when Con Agra developed the *bold* version they attempted to sell to grown up tastes, then I found a new low-fat way of enjoying a childhood tradition.

Ingredients:

- 1 pound 96/4 % ground beef
- 1 can of *bold* Manwhich sauce
- 1 tomato

- yellow mustard
- Borden fat free cheese slice
- light mayonnaise

Method:

1. Brown beef, drain in colander and rinse. Add Sloppy Joe sauce.
2. In a small cup mix 1 tablespoon of light mayonnaise with 2 tablespoons of yellow mustard and stir.

3. Spread on a toasted hamburger bun, add 1 tomato slice and one slice of cheese.

Chinese (non) Fried Rice

Chinese Fried Rice, a common take-out dish is often combined with leftover meats and vegetables and then fried to become a new dish called Chinese Chicken and Fried Rice. In this recipe we skip the oils and the frying while maintaining the taste.

Ingredients:

- ½ cup of egg substitute
- 2 cups of rice
- 32 oz of chicken broth
- chopped green onion
- non-fat cooking spray

- 1 teaspoon of onion powder
- 2 cloves of chopped garlic
- 2 tablespoon of soy sauce
- pinch of Accent brand seasoning (optional)

Optional Ingredients for Chicken Fried Rice

- 1 pound skinless, boneless chicken breasts
- 1 tablespoon of soy sauce

- 2 teaspoons of McCormick's *Far East Ginger and Sesame Blend Seasoning*

Method:

1. Place rice, broth, soy sauce, garlic, salt, pepper, Accent and onion powder in small pan and bring to a boil over medium-high heat.
2. Stir, cover and reduce heat to medium-low and cook for 18 minutes.
3. In a separate frying pan sprayed with cooking spray, scramble egg substitute.
4. After the 18 minutes, remove lid, stir in egg, chopped onions then fluff with a fork.
5. If making Chicken Fried Rice then, cook chicken using non-fat spray, adding in seasoning and soy sauce. Then mix chicken with rice and serve.

Chicken Yakisoba

Chicken Yakisoba

One night in London we happened upon a lovely take-out Chinese & Japanese noodle house near Jubilee Gardens. There we ordered Yakisoba chicken, and took it over to a bench a few feet from the Thames river, where we sat under the glow of the London Eye and the clock tower at Westminster Palace (Big Ben). What more could a girl ask for?

Ingredients:

- 1 pound of skinless chicken breast
- ½ sweet onion
- 1 handful of bok choi (Chinese cabbage)
- 1 teaspoon of Worcestershire sauce
- ½ cup of egg substitute
- 1 box of wheat thin spaghetti

- 3 tablespoons of soy sauce
- 2 tablespoons of Teriyaki sauce
- 1 package of Portobello mushrooms
- 2 teaspoons of McCormick's brand *Far East Sesame & Ginger Blend*
- Non-fat cooking spray
- pinch of Accent brand seasoning (optional)

Method:

1. Chop chicken, onions, mushrooms and shred bok choi.
2. Cook chicken using non-fat spray, adding in vegetables near completion.
3. Cook eggs in separate frying pan with spray.
4. Boil water and cook noodles to firm per box.
5. Strain noodles.
6. Shut off heat, spray pot with spray, and return noodles to pot.
7. Add to the noodles, seasonings, and sauces. Mix well with tongs.
8. Add chicken and vegetables.
9. Continue mixing, as you add cooked eggs.

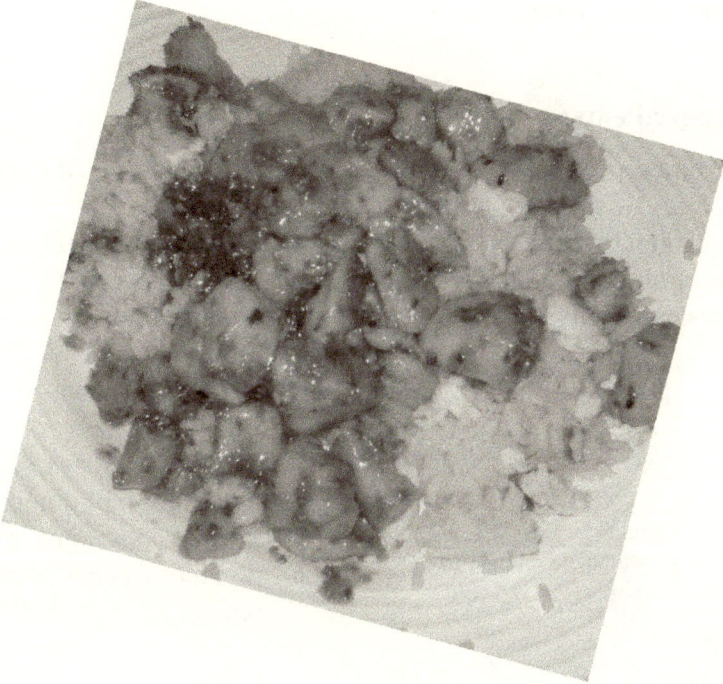

Chinese Sesame Chicken

Chinese Sesame Chicken

Probably one of our favorite Chinese dishes is sesame chicken. While I was in the process of making other Chinese dishes, it only made sense to include this one. My apologies to the local Chinese restaurant which we won't be visiting anymore.

Ingredients:

- Chinese rice (page: 94)
- 16 oz. of skinless, boneless chicken breasts
- non-fat cooking spray
- sesame seeds
- 1 tablespoons of raspberry wine
- 3 tablespoons of honey
- 3 tablespoons of sugar
- 1 tablespoon of rice vinegar
- 2 teaspoons of McCormick's brand *Far East Sesame & Ginger blend*
- 1 teaspoon of soy sauce
- ½ teaspoon of ginger
- ½ teaspoon of garlic powder
- pinch of Accent brand seasoning (optional)

Method:

1. Prepare rice.
2. Chop chicken into cubes.
3. Cook chicken in pan with non-fat cooking spray
4. When chicken is cooked, add wine, honey, soy sauce, vinegar, *Far East* seasonings, sugar, garlic and ginger.
5. Toss quickly over medium-high heat as mixture reduces to a glaze.
6. Plate and top with sesame seeds. Serving with rice.

Katsudon

Katsudon is a traditional Japanese comfort food typically served with pork which has become a favorite in our home. It can also be made with battered chicken or beef.

Ingredients:

- pork tenderloin
- ¼ teaspoon of black pepper
- 1 cup breadcrumbs
- 1 cup beef broth
- 4 tablespoons of mirin
- 1 onion sliced thin
- Chinese rice (page: 94)
- pinch of salt
- 1 cup flour
- 1¼ cup of egg substitute
- 6 tablespoons of soy sauce
- chives
- non-fat cooking spray

Method:

1. Cook rice.

2. Flour, egg and batter thin patties of pork tenderloin in ¼ cup of egg substitute.

3. Using non-fat cooking spray sweat onion slices, and cook breaded pork.

4. Transfer pork to oven sheet and finish cooking at 350° F.

5. Boil onion, beef broth, mirin and soy sauce.

6. Remove from heat. Add remaining egg. As egg solidifies, but before it completely hardens, fill a table bowl with rice, place one meat piece on top, and pour broth and egg mixture over top. Garnish with chives.

Cincinnati Style Chili Mac

I had my first Cincinnati chili-mac dish at the Cincinnati airport on a connecting flight to Los Angeles a few years back. From that point on, I was hooked. Like the Philadelphia cheesesteak, Cincinnati's claim to fame has produced rival variations of the chili-mac dish: Skyline and Gold Star.

Chili on spaghetti originated in 1922 when a hot dog vendor by the name Tom Kiradijeff took his traditional family stew from Macedonia and sold it on top of traditional spaghetti noodles.

Cincinnati chili is ordered by saying "one way", (basic bowl of chili) "two way", etc... with "six way" including chili, pasta, sauce, cheese, onions and garlic; but may include, beans, and jalapeños.

Ingredients:

- thin spaghetti
- Cabot 75 cheese
- Liv's meal chili (page: 64)
- chopped onions

Method:

1. Boil water.

2. Cook spaghetti.

3. Prepare chili

4. Grate cheese, top generously on top of spaghetti and chili.

5. Garnish with chopped onions.

Enchiladas & Mexican Rice

Enchiladas

Enchiladas are a popular Mexican dish which uses tortillas dipped in a tomato based sauce and baked. Originally a finger food where a flat bread was dipped in a sauce, the dish evolved into the baked dish it is when people began stuffing and rolling the tortillas similar the cabbage and olive wrapped dishes of Europe.

Ingredients:

- 1 pound skinless chicken breasts
- salsa caliente (page: 53)
- 2- 8 oz. packages of Cabot 75 cheese
- non-fat cooking spray
- tortillas
- ½ onion chopped
- cilantro to taste
- Mexican rice (as side) (page: 50)

Method:

1. Chop chicken and onion and grill on stove with non-stick spray.

2. Transfer to bowl. Add 8 oz of cheese, chopped cilantro, and 1 cup of salsa then mix..

3. Take warmed tortillas and add filling. Roll, and place in large baking pan which has been sprayed with non-fat cooking spray.

4. Take additional amounts of salsa and top rolled enchiladas.

5. Take second block of cheese, shred, and top over sauce.

6. Bake for 20 minutes in a 350° F preheated oven.

7. Serve with lettuce, tomato, and sour cream.

3 Cheese Macaroni, Sausage and Sauerkraut

I can't pinpoint why, but for some reason sausage and kraut with macaroni and cheese just goes together. It's a traditional southern dish which entices its eater to mix it all up and eat it.

There is some historical consequence to it all. Sauerkraut is a typical German relish which was brought to America by immigrants and served as a garnish on sausage or whatever leftovers may have been laying around the kitchen. Somewhere along the line, someone had the brilliant idea to take the previous nights' macaroni and toss it in a casserole with some sausage and kraut.

Ingredients:

- 1 can of non Bavarian sauerkraut
- ¼ cup of water
- 1 8 oz package of Cabot 75 cheese
- 1 16 oz box of elbow macaroni
- 1 package of smoked turkey dinner sausage
- bread crumbs
- 1 package Velveeta 2% cheese
- 1 24 oz container of fat-free cottage cheese

Method:

1. Chunk sausage and cook, adding drained sauerkraut ¾ way through.
2. Boil and drain elbow macaroni.
3. Chop Velveeta into small blocks.
4. Shred Cabot cheese.
5. With heat off mix noodles and all cheeses.
6. Pour macaroni and cheese into large baking pan and sprinkle with bread crumbs.
7. Bake in preheated oven at 350° F for about 20 minutes.

Mojo Burritos

The word burrito which translates to *little donkey* is derived from the appearance of the wrapped up tortilla and its visual similarity to a donkey's ear.

While new-age burrito restaurants litter the fast food landscape now, the one thing they can't give you is the real secret ingredient to true Mexican cuisine: family. Being able to build a massive home-made burrito with unlimited toppings, drink a nice cold cerveza, listen to music and socialize with family all the while enjoying one of the best meals you've ever had, that's my idea of a meal.

Ingredients:

- 2 pounds of top round, London broil, or boneless skinless chicken breasts.
- 2 tablespoons of corn oil (optional)
- salsa (page: 44)
- warmed tortillas
- tomatoes and lettuce
- ½ cups of Goya brand MOJO criollo
- 2 batches of burrito seasoning (page: 60)
- Mexican rice (page: 50)
- fat free sour cream
- Cabot 75 brand cheese

Method:

1. Chunk raw meat and place in zippered plastic bag with Mojo marinate and seasoning. Marinate well in cold refrigerator for one hour. When ready to use discard additional marinade.

2. Preheat pan to medium high heat, add corn oil then grill meat.

3. Assemble burrito with shredded cheese, rice, salsa, and any other additional toppings.

Grandma's Chicken Soup

Grandma Hendrickson was famous for her chicken soup. If you were sick, dying, or even just hungry and cold you usually ended up with a huge bowl of the stuff. One time I inquired what laundry list of secret ingredients may be necessary to reproduce such a timely classic and Grandma said "salt and pepper." Well, today I still make it pretty much the same. A few extra key ingredients that I learned along the way, make this recipe a refined and polished chicken soup recipe.

Ingredients:

- 1 49.5 oz can of chicken broth
- 1 teaspoon salt
- 1 teaspoon paprika
- 1 teaspoon of black pepper
- ¾ teaspoon of Tabasco hot sauce
- 1 bag of egg noodles
- ½ onion chopped
- 4 cloves of minced garlic
- 1 large egg
- 1 pound boneless skinless chicken breasts

Method:

1. In a large pot, cook noodles and drain in colander.

2. Pour broth into drained pot, add garlic, Tabasco, pepper, onion, paprika and bring to boil.

3. Reduce heat, quickly add one egg and whisk vigorously. Finally add back in noodles.

4. Chop and grill chicken and onions on stove top and add to soup.

French Onion Soup

It seems like everyone has a French onion soup recipe. It's not as simple as one might think, especially when the core to French cooking is butter, but I think you'll find this low-fat version is just as remarkable as its fattier alternatives. I really felt the Gruyère cheese although it is high in fat, was a necessity for authenticity. However feel free to replace with a low-fat cheese of your choice or shred lightly to reduce fat content even more.

Ingredients:

- 1 32 oz box of chicken broth
- 1 teaspoon salt
- 1 teaspoon balsamic vinegar
- ½ teaspoon of black pepper
- 8 oz Gruyère cheese
- ½ cup of cooking sherry
- 14.5 oz beef broth (1 can)
- 1 yellow onion chopped
- 1 baguette sliced
- 1 tablespoon fat-free sour cream
- 2 oz of roast beef chopped
- 4 cloves of minced garlic

Method:

1. Chop garlic, roast beef, and onions and place in large pot over medium high heat. Add ½ cup a sherry, salt pepper, vinegar, and stir until reduced and onions are softened. Add beef and chicken broth then increase heat to high and bring to a boil while stirring.

2. Once boiling, shut burner off and add one tablespoon of fat-free sour cream while whisking vigorously.

3. Ladle into bowls.

4. Take 2 ½ inch slices of baguette bread and lay on top. Top with cheese. Ladle one more spoon full over cheese.

Chicken Diablo

Chicken Diablo

This simple, spicy chicken recipe is not only terrific but also low-fat. Add your favorite chilled beer, and you've got the perfect bar food indulgence for watching the soccer match on television, or another flavorful dinner idea with no need for remorse.

These go great with the stuffed jalapeños that I mention later in the book or even some Mexican rice to make it a full-fledged dinner.

Ingredients:

- skinless boneless chicken breasts
- center cut bacon
- 8 ounce of fat-free sour cream
- cilantro
- chipotle peppers in Adobo Sauce
- Cabot 75 cheese
- pickled jalapeños

Method:

1. Butterfly cut your chicken breasts.

2. Fill with bacon slices, and jalapeños.

3. Bake on non-stick, sprayed cookie sheet at 350° F for 1 hour total, flipping over half-way through.

4. Top with cheese about 10 minutes from completion.

5. Take 1 chipotle pepper and sour cream and food process.

6. Top chicken with pepper-cream and garnish with cilantro.

Boneless Ranch Chicken Wing Sandwich

I love this sandwich which combines the heat of buffalo chicken wings with creamy ranch sauce together on a thrilling sandwich. You can also use this recipe to make wing style boneless chicken.

Make it even healthier by skipping the breading all together, and you'll realize the breading is more of a texture than a taste.

Ingredients:

- breadcrumbs
- boneless skinless chicken breasts or strips
- hamburger buns
- fat free ranch dressing
- egg substitute
- Frank's original hot sauce
- lettuce and tomatoes
- pickled jalapeños

Method:

1. Take two freezer size zippered plastic bags. Fill one with breadcrumbs, and one with egg substitute.

2. Butterfly cut chicken (or slice for wing style) and batter.

3. Fry on stove top using non-fat spray till golden brown.

4. Bake chicken on cooking sheet for about 25 minutes at 350° F or until cooked thoroughly.

5. Remove from oven, and dip in bowl of hot sauce.

6. Place on bun top with tomato and lettuce, spread ranch on top of bun and add a few Jalapeños.

Cuban Coca

This is one of those super simple recipes. It's also very healthy. If we made it in Italy it would be a type of *white pizza* because it has no red sauce. It's a simple pizza-like bread topped with smoked turkey sausage and red onion that's common place in Cuba.

Spice it up a bit by adding Roma tomatoes, asparagus, portobello mushrooms, red peppers, even drizzle with honey, or try goat cheese. The variations are endless!

Ingredients:

- Coca Loca recipe (page: 144)
- 1 package of smoked turkey dinner sausage
- 1 red onion, chopped
- ¼ cup water
- a pinch of each: salt, pepper, and garlic powder

Method:

1. Produce coca bread per instructions, but do not bake.
2. Slice sausage into large chunks.
3. Place onion and sausage in fry pan with water.
4. On high heat cook till water has evaporated and onions caramelize. Season with salt, pepper, and garlic powder.
5. Top coca bread, and place in oven at 450° F for 10-12 minutes.

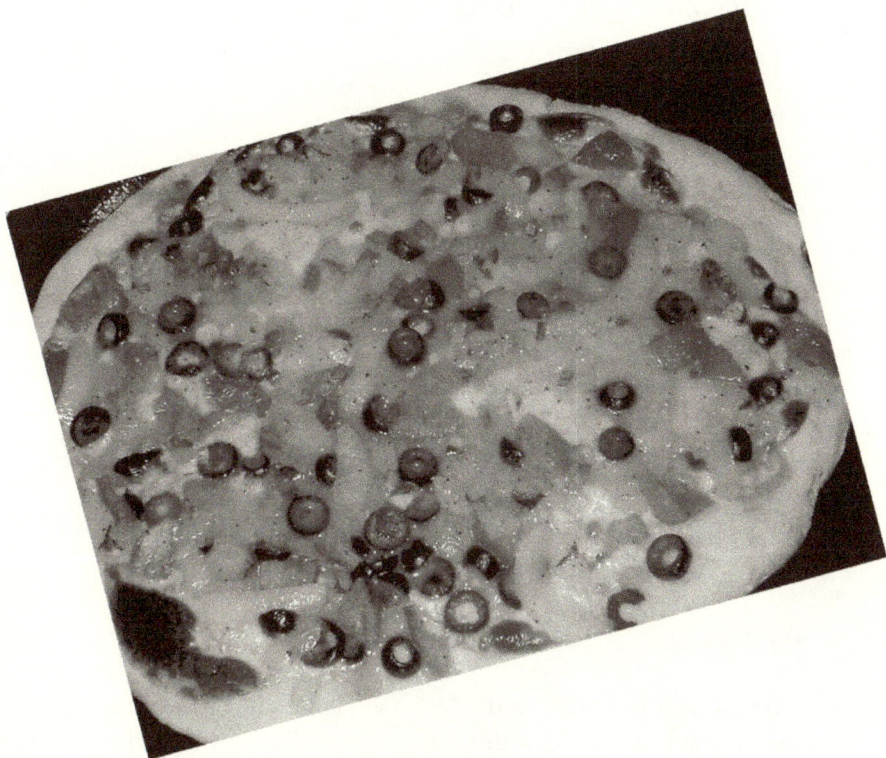

Pissaladière

Pissaladière

Pissaladière like Cuban coca is a white pizza but from south France. Traditional Pissaladière uses the flavors of anchovies, thyme and black olives upon a open face tart. This version uses a low-fat vinaigrette to provide a familiar taste without the fat.

Ingredients:

- 2.5 cups of bread flour
- 1 packet of rapid rise yeast

- 2 teaspoons of chopped green onion

- ½ cup sliced black olives

- 1 chopped onion
- ½ teaspoon of garlic powder

- 1 cup + 1 tablespoon of cold water
- ½ teaspoon of salt
- ½ teaspoon of sugar

- 4 oz. low-fat provolone cheese

- ½ cup of low-fat Cesar dressing (vinaigrette)
- 1 chopped tomato
- 2 teaspoons of chopped fresh thyme

Method:

1. Mix flour, salt, sugar and yeast in a bowl. Add water and knead dough for 8-10 minutes.
2. Preheat oven to 200°F, then shut off. Place dough in glass or metal bowl sprayed with non-fat cooking spray and cover with tin-foil. Place in oven for 45 minutes to rise.

- Heat chopped onions with fat-free spray and a pinch of salt and pepper.
- Transfer to a bowl and add thyme, tomato, olives, and garlic. Mix well.
- Place dough on baking sheet, and top with provolone, and other ingredients, garnish with green onions.
- Bake in preheated oven at 450° F for 10-12 minutes.

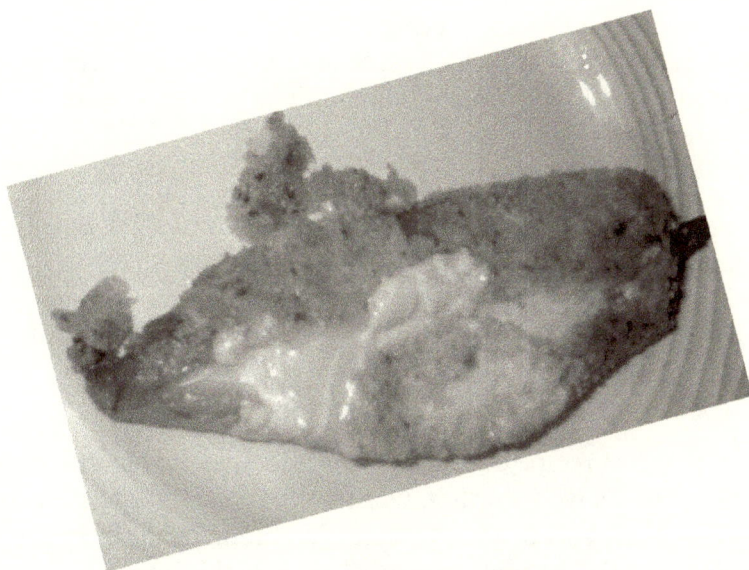

Chile Rellenos

Chiles Rellenos

For all the gringos (non Spanish speaking) out there, chiles rellenos is nothing more than the Mexican take on stuffed peppers. Rellenos translated means: filling, or stuffing. One of our family's favorites, this easy recipe makes a nutritious snack, meal or side-dish. This version uses only queso (cheese), but you can also add beef (carne), or chicken (pollo), as well as carne asada (steak) and carnitas (roast), along with tomatoes and onions into the cheese filling if you so choose.

When shopping for chiles, look for a thick fleshed, straight chile large enough to hold the rellenos. Yes, the Anaheim peppers used in this recipe were named for the city of Anaheim, California. Poblanos are also a popular and the traditional pepper for chile rellenos, and is named after Puebla, a city near Mexico City. Do not use bell peppers.

This recipe does take a considerable amount of time, but it's well worth it. Our family typically eats chiles without any sort of sauce, but it is common to serve with a salsa, like those mentioned previously in this book.

Chiles Rellenos

Ingredients:

- California green chiles (also known as Anaheim peppers)
- Cabot 75 cheese

- sour cream and salsa
- 1 package fat free cream cheese.

- 1 teaspoon of olive oil for each pepper
- flour, egg substitute and breadcrumbs for battering
- tin foil

Method:

1. Preheat oven to 450°F

2. Turn stove top to medium-high, and scorch the outside of peppers (yes burn, till black) directly on element or flame with no pan.

3. Rinse peppers and scrape burnt skin off with edge of knife.

4. Make vertical incision in peppers, de-seed. (gloves are helpful)

5. Mix cream cheese and shredded Cabot Cheese in bowl, and stuff into peppers and close.

6. Roll pepper in flour, egg (substitute) and batter peppers.

7. Place each battered pepper on a square of tin-foil and drizzle each with 1 teaspoon of olive oil. Tent foil and loosely crimp close the ends upwards to prevent the oil from leaking.

8. Bake for 15 minutes in oven

9. Remove from oven, plate immediately, (opening with tongs of course) and garnish with sour cream and salsa.

L.A. Style French Dip

The French dip sandwich originated far from France in the city of Los Angeles around 1918 when restaurant owner Philippe Mathieu, accidentally dropped his customer's bun in the meat juice. Next thing you know, people are clamoring for the French dip, a sandwich born and made till this day in the city of Angels.

Ingredients:

- 1 14.5 oz can of chicken broth
- 1 packet of McCormick's brand au jus mix.
- 1¼ cup of water
- shredded Gruyère cheese

- French bread
- 1 sweet onion
- 1 pound of sliced roast beef
- pinches of salt, pepper and garlic powder to taste
- non-fat cooking spray

Method:

1. Pour broth, water and au jus seasoning in a pan and bring to a boil while whisking, then reduce heat and simmer.

2. Sweat chopped onions on medium high heat with spray adding chopped beef then au jus mix.

3. Season to taste then take bread and cut into open face sandwich. Float the inside portion of the bottom and top bun on top of the au jus allowing it to soak up the sauce.

4. Spoon meat and onions on to the bun, top with cheese.

Snacker Burgers

When the inventors of the hamburger stumbled upon the
technique of flattening a meatball and placing it on a bun
to allow customers a portable method for eating meatballs,
this is probably what they envisioned:

Ingredients:
- 1 tube of refrigerated French bread dough
- fresh mushrooms
- 1 onion
- A-1 steak sauce
- lettuce and tomato
- 1 pound 96/4 % ground beef
- Cabot 75 cheese or Borden fat free slices
- ¼ pound center cut bacon
- Lea & Perrin's Worcestershire sauce

Method:
1. Take dough and cut into 12 cookie like dough sections.
2. Bake for 9 minutes.
3. Place beef in mixing bowl.
4. Chop uncooked onion, mushrooms & bacon then mix with beef.
5. Take 1 tablespoon of Worcestershire sauce and mix with beef.
6. Form 8 patties and place on wax paper on top of a cutting board. Freeze patties for 10-15 minutes.
7. Cook over medium high.
8. Place meat patties on bun and top with cheese and A1 sauce.

Vegetarian Mushroom Burger

If you've ever tried to be vegetarian but didn't think you could do it then try these. It's one of our favorites, and topped with A-1, it's a zesty little treat that doesn't really make us miss real meat all that very much. I may always be a part-time vegetarian, but I'm always amazed by how good things can taste when they're not covered up by fat.

Ingredients:

- large (giant) Portobello mushrooms
- A-1 brand sauce
- onions
- fat-free cooking spray
- hamburger buns

Method:

1. Slice onions.

2. With a spoon, scoop out black underbelly of mushrooms and dispose.

3. Rinse and then cook mushrooms with non-fat spray thoroughly on stove top.

4. Saute onions for a few minutes with patties, and then place both on bun.

5. Top generously with A-1 and enjoy.

Hunky Drip in Grandpa's Garage

A family get-together celebrated with pork drippings over
fire, the hunky drip was an important part of growing up in
our family.

(Kimberly, Aunt Rose, & Uncle Dave)

Hunky Drip

Growing up in an area of Hungarian and German residents, my family would always celebrate festive holidays by having what they called a *hunky drip*. Basically it involves a huge chunk of jowl pork (a big slab of a pig,) scored like a grid with a knife and heated over an open fire till the fat melts, at which time you would drip the grease onto your bread and add vegetables. The crisped fat would then be cut off and added to the sandwich. Here's a much healthier version:

Ingredients:

- sourdough bread
- chopped onions
- low-fat margarine
- garlic powder, black pepper and salt
- chopped green peppers
- salt and pepper
- center cut bacon
- fat free cooking spray

Method:

1. Cook and crisp bacon.

2. Saute chopped onions, peppers with salt and pepper in fat-free spray.

3. Take slice of bread and butter 1 side.

4. Fry face down, topping with bacon and vegetables.

5. Fold in half, eat.

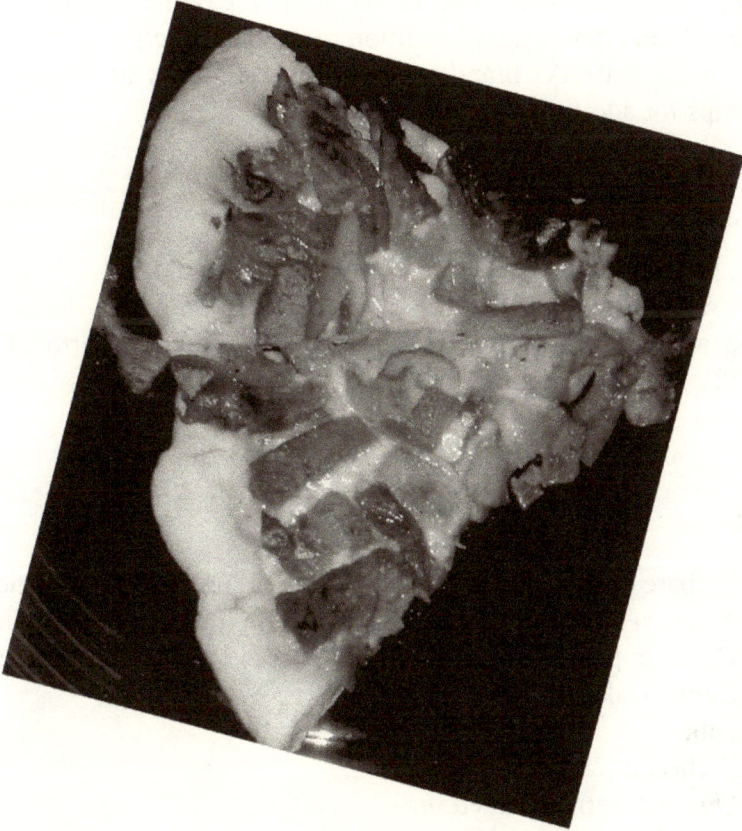

London Steak Special Pizza

London Steak Special Pizza

This is a great sauce-less white pizza similar to a Philly cheesesteak but on a pizza instead. Named for the style of the cut of beef used: London broil, it's the perfect flavors in a brand new way. In addition to the basic recipe, you can add some A1 brand steak sauce or HP sauce in dipping cups for additional flavor.

Ingredients:

- 2 pizza doughs (page: 57)
- low fat provolone cheese
- steakhouse seasonings (page: 48)
- top round or London broil
- 1 red onion
- 1 package of Portobello mushrooms

Method:

1. Prepare dough, and layout on pizza sheet.
2. Cover in provolone.
3. Chop steak into small cubes.
4. Preheat oven to 450° F
5. On stove top over medium-high heat cook steak, onions and mushrooms and seasonings.
6. Strain meat and veggies.
7. Top pizzas with toppings.
8. Bake for 10-12 minutes.

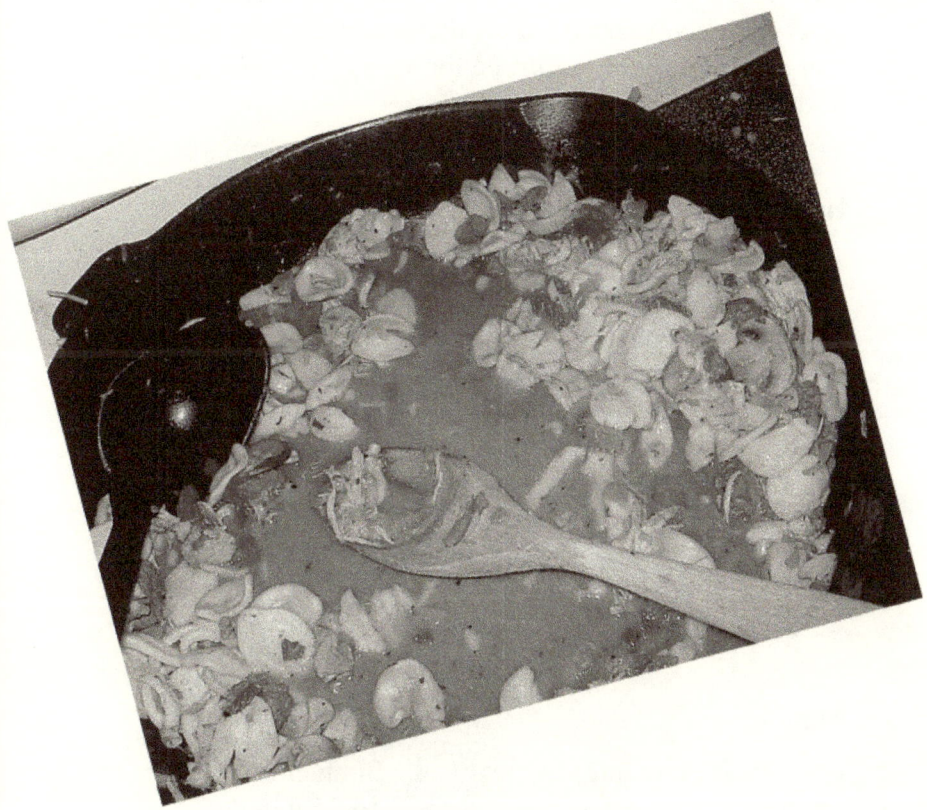

Fat Boy's Gordo Rose Pasta

Fat Boy's Gordo Rose Pasta

Here's a recipe that will use up the left-over wine in the
rack, and is made up of just a few odds and ends in the
pantry; but, will create a meal that will make you feel like
you hopped a flight to Europe for a very expensive candle
lit dinner.

Ingredients:

- 1 pkg Orecchiette pasta, boiled and drained
- 1 package of spicy turkey sausage links de-tubed and crumbled.
- 1 14.5 oz can of chicken broth
- 1-2 cups Spanish Porto red wine.
- 2-3 oz of sun dried tomato halves (chopped)
- 1 package of portobello mushrooms
- 1 red onion (chopped)
- 6 cloves of garlic (chopped)
- salt, pepper & spice
- Parmesan cheese

Method:

1. Cook meat and saute veggies on stove top.
2. Boil and drain pasta.
3. Combine all, add wine & broth.
4. Simmer on medium heat for 10-15 minutes.
5. Top with cheese and serve.

NOSH!
THE INTERNATIONAL DIET COOKBOOK
Breakfast Recipes

Banana and Cinnamon French Toast

This is an amazing recipe for French toast with the best part that it's completely fat-free, except for the butter you may choose to place on top. Serve with a few fresh strawberries, and you'll never miss a single gram of fat.

If you need a recommendation for your first recipe to try in this book, this is it. It's amazingly mind blowing. It's so good you'll probably lift your nose in disgust at anyone else's French toast that you're served in the future.

Ingredients:
- Banana Nutter Bread (page: 159)
- fat-free cooking spray
- nutmeg
- vanilla extract
- cinnamon powder
- egg substitute
- low-fat butter or margarine
- light syrup

Method:
1. Cut bread into slices.
2. Pour egg substitute with nutmeg, vanilla, & cinnamon to taste in shallow plate.
3. Dip both sides of bread in egg mix.
4. Spray frying pan with non-stick spray.
5. Fry each side of bread.
6. Serve with a dollop of low-fat butter, and light syrup.
7. Garnish with sliced bananas.

Breakfast Burritos

A few years ago, after moving back to the East Coast I realized how much I was missing my breakfast burritos which are common place in California but non-existent at the time out here.

Luckily things have changed, but during that period the only place I could get one was my own kitchen. Today I still make them at home, because the commercially available ones are not nearly as good, and much higher in fat.

Ingredients:
- tortillas
- pinch of Catalina spice mix (less than 1/8 teaspoon)
- Cabot 75 cheese (shredded)
- chopped red ripe tomatoes
- egg substitute
- shredded lettuce
- center cut bacon (or turkey bacon)
- fat free sour cream
- Liv's salsa.

Method:
1. Warm tortilla in microwave about 10 seconds.
2. Mix eggs and spice mix.
3. Cook eggs using non-fat cooking spray.
4. Fry bacon (draining grease if using center cut).
5. Place eggs into tortilla, add tomatoes, lettuce, bacon, cheese, sour cream, and salsa.
6. Roll into tortilla and grill seam side down in frying pan till slightly crisp. Flip, repeat, and eat.

Quiche

Quiche, traditionally is a French derived, open faced pie filled with egg custard, meats and vegetables. You might think it's a breakfast only dish based on the ingredients, but it's great anytime. Hot or cold.

Ingredients:

- whole grain bread
- ½ pound turkey bacon
- mushrooms
- 2 cups Cabot 75 cheese shredded
- salt and pepper to taste
- egg substitute
- ½ pound of low-fat ground turkey sausage
- 1 chopped onion
- 1 chopped tomato

Method:

1. Preheat oven to 350° F

2. Cook and crumble bacon and turkey.

3. Take several pieces of bread (enough to cover bottom of a 13x9 cooking pan) and remove edges.

4. Coat pan with non-fat cooking spray and lay bread on bottom of pan to form flat surface.

5. Pour egg substitute in pan over bread.

6. Add meats, 1 cup of cheese, sliced onions and mushrooms evenly to pan.

7. Bake at 350° F until eggs are cooked.

8. Remove from oven and coat with second cup of cheese and chopped tomatoes.

Chili Cheese Omelet

Chili cheese omelets are a great morning after breakfast
when you had chili-burgers the night before. Sometimes I
freeze chili in little individual tubs and save some
precisely for making the perfect omelet. If your chili is
already prepared, it's literally a 10 minute meal.

Ingredients:

- Liv's low fat chili
- egg substitute
- fat-free cheese slices
- chopped onions
- chopped tomatoes
- non-fat cooking spray
- salt & pepper to taste

Method:

1. Coat non-stick omelet pan with non-fat cooking spray. Add onions, and warm for about a minute.

2. Add in enough egg substitute to fill bottom of pan

3. Sprinkle some black pepper. Add warmed (or just made) chili onto omelet and cover with two slices of cheese.

4. Add chopped tomatoes, move to plate and eat.

Chili Breakfast Sandwich

When I said this wasn't your ordinary recipe book, I wasn't kidding. It seems unbelievable you can have foods like chili sausage sandwiches for breakfast and still lose weight, but you can. First you'll need to prepare some of my chili. Commonly I'll freeze some after a cookout, and then pull it out in the morning for some delicious chili breakfast sandwiches. Don't knock the idea if you've never had them. They're a huge hit in Los Angeles, at a restaurant called Tommy's. Yes I'd love to take credit, but I must reference Tommy Koulax as the person who invented the world's best fast-food breakfast. My low-fat version now makes it safe to eat one without needing to visit a cardiologist afterwards.

Ingredients:
- English muffins
- egg substitute
- pickles
- sliced tomatoes
- low fat ground turkey sausage
- fat-free cheese slices.
- chopped onions
- condiment chili (page: 63)

Method:
1. Make and cook sausage patties,cook egg substitute, and warm the chili.
2. Add a generous proportion of chili on to the top of the muffin, top with cheese pickle, onion, and tomatoes.

The Steak Bagel Breakfast

Here's a recipe for a simple steak bagel. It's a great high protein breakfast which goes great with anything. Your use of steak will ultimately effect your fat count. A very thin cut is your best option.

Ingredients:

- very thinly cut top sirloin.
- pinch of steakhouse seasoning blend (page: 48)
- egg substitute
- chopped red onion
- fat-free cheese slice or fat-free cream cheese
- red onion
- fat-free cooking spray
- wheat bagels

Method:

1. Cook steak and onions to medium-well, sprinkling with a pinch of steakhouse seasoning on a sprayed non-stick span.

2. Scramble egg substitute with non-fat spray.

3. Toast bagel.

4. Take bagel and assemble with cheese, steak, onions, and eggs.

Scotch Eggs

Scotch Eggs

Contrary to its name, Scotch eggs weren't invented in Scotland, but by the British in 1851 at a London restaurant called Fortnum and Mason.

Traditionally deep-fried, this recipe saves a ton on fat and calories by using 4.5 gram per serving turkey sausage, and baking the dish rather than deep frying.

Ingredients:

- 8 large Eggs
- 2 pounds of turkey sausage
- egg substitute
- breadcrumbs
- non-fat cooking spray
- HP Sauce or A1 sauce

Method:

1. Hard boil eggs.
2. Remove shells and allow to cool.
3. Wrap in sausage.
4. Dip in egg substitute.
5. Cover in breadcrumbs.
6. Place on baking sheet coated with cooking spray.
7. Bake for 30 minutes at 350° F.
8. Cut in half, drizzle with HP sauce or A1, and enjoy.

NOSH!
THE INTERNATIONAL DIET COOKBOOK
Side Dish Recipes

Poutine

Poutine is a Canadian comfort food generally made with cheese curds. If you've never had Poutine then I can clearly tell you, you've not lived yet. Making it low-fat as I have is probably against national Canadian law, but you will fall in love with this food just as my son Chance has, as well as our entire family.

Ingredients:
- fast food style baked French fries (page: 61)
- 1 Au jus seasoning pack
- 1 tablespoon of flour
- light mozzarella cheese
- salt to taste

Method:
1. Bake French fries in oven.
2. Remove from oven and place fries in bowl, cover in light mozzarella cheese and allow to melt.
3. Take au jus packet, and boil with water, adding flour to thicken as necessary.
4. Take ladle and pour over cheese and fries.

Jalapeño Poppers

We put a little twist on this Super Bowl favorite: bacon.
Best of all it's low-fat, and healthier than the deep-fried,
breaded alternatives. You might want to pick up a pair of
gloves, as jalapeños can irritate both skin and eyes.

QUICK FACTS:

- Also known as Armadillo eggs, Texas torpedoes, jalapeño slammers, and atomic buffalo turds. (ABTs)

- Originated from France and called croquettes, (from the French *croquer*, "to eat hastily") traditional versions are basically meat, vegetable, or potato encased in breadcrumbs and fried.

- The word jalapeño (xalapeno) comes from the city name Xalapa, Veracruz Mexico.

- Jalapeños are picked before they're ripened. jalapeños which become red are often discarded as inferior peppers.

Jalapeño Poppers

Ingredients:
- jalapeños.
- Cabot 75 sharp cheddar cheese
- fat free cream cheese
- low-fat turkey sausage
- tooth picks
- center cut bacon

Method:

1. Preheat oven to 325°F
2. Cut the tops of the jalapeño Peppers, using a knife, remove the seeds.
3. In a bowl, combine 1/2 roll of sausage, and 1/2 bag of your Cabot cheese.
4. Stuff into pepper cavities leaving 1/4 of the total body empty.
5. Wrap and toothpick the pepper in 1/2 length of center cut bacon strips.
6. Place on pan (cupcake pan works great!) and bake for about 15 minutes.
7. Remove from oven, and fill the remainder of the peppers with cream cheese. Place back in oven and cook for another 15+ minutes. Peppers are done when bacon is cooked, and cream cheese in browned on top.

Stuffed Mushrooms

This is a simple, and tasty side-dish that goes well with a hearty home-cooked meal. It's versatile and can be served with steak and potatoes, Italian cuisine or merely an appetizer for something else.

Ingredients:

- fresh whole mushrooms
- 10 oz can of crushed tomatoes
- Salt and pepper
- Cabot 75 cheese

- low-fat ground turkey sausage
- 1 teaspoon of chopped garlic
- bread crumbs

Method:

1. Wash mushrooms and remove stems.

2. In a bowl, mix sausage and cheese.

3. Fill mushrooms.

4. Place in deep baking pan.

5. Crumble breadcrumbs over top.

6. Bake for 5 minutes at 350° F

7. Food process mushroom stems with crushed tomatoes, and garlic. Salt and pepper to taste.

8. Remove from oven and pour sauce over mushroom tops.

9. Return to oven for and additional 15-20 minutes or until sausage is cooked.

Deluxe Taco Cheese Fries

Here's another that came out of necessity. You can't buy
these on the East Coast, but are inexplicably addictive.
They go great with hamburgers, tacos, or as a meal by
themselves.

Ingredients:

- 1 pound of 96/4 % ground beef
- taco seasoning (page: 60)
- 1 onion
- 1 tomato
- fat free sour cream
- Cabot 75 cheese
- fast food style French fries (page: 61)

Method:

1. Brown ground beef, drain in colander and rinse. Return to skillet add seasonings and water, and simmer.

2. Bake fries, and place on plate. Add taco meat, shredded cheese onions, tomatoes and garnish with sour cream.

Mile High Twice Baked Potatoes (6 count)

No more flat baked potatoes. The trick is the extra one.

Ingredients:

- 7 potatoes
- ½ cup of fat-free sour cream
- ½ teaspoon of salt
- 1/8 teaspoon of black pepper
- chives
- 1 small container of fat-free cream cheese
- 1 tablespoon of Butter Buds
- ½ teaspoon of all-season salt
- 2 tablespoons of low-fat margarine

Method:

1. Peel 1 potato.
2. Take the 6 un-peeled and 1 peeled potato and microwave on high for 10 minutes, flip and microwave for an additional 10 minutes.
3. Set peeled potato aside.
4. Take knife and remove the very top of the 6 potatoes. (about ¼ inch) *Don't cut in half! 90/10 Cut.
5. Scoop insides out with spoon.
6. Microwave low-fat butter, and with pastry brush glaze potato cavities.
7. Sprinkle insides with salt, and place scooped potatoes aside in a bowl.
8. Place empty skins in preheated oven at 375° F for 15 minutes.
9. Mash insides adding extra potato, salt, pepper, sour cream, Butter Buds, and cheese. Mix thoroughly
10. When skins have cooked for 15 minutes, remove and stuff till they're a mile high.
11. Bake an additional 15 minutes, garnish with chives and enjoy!

Baked Buñuelos de Queso

Buñuelos are a Mexican fritter and are generally fried.
This recipe (a cheese fritter) allows the same great taste,
without all the fat of deep-frying.

Ingredients:

- 2 cups flour
- 1/3 cup fat-free buttermilk
- 4 teaspoon baking powder
- ½ teaspoon salt
- 1 teaspoon sugar
- ¾ cup of plain non-fat yogurt (or 1 6oz single serving)
- ½ cup of low-fat butter or margarine
- 1 cup of shredded Cabot 75 cheese.

Method:

1. Preheat oven to 450° F.
2. Mix salt, sugar, flour, and baking powder in a bowl.
3. Stir in yogurt, butter, cheese and milk.
4. Mix well.
5. Take heaping tablespoons of dough and place on fat-free sprayed baking sheet.
6. Bake for 7 minutes.

Vegetarian Nachos

Occasionally meat in general will be very expensive.
Rather than spending lots of money on meat, we will just
wait a week and make vegetarian dishes in the meantime.
This one is so great, I really don't even miss the meat.

Ingredients:

- 2% light Velveeta cheese product
- chopped onions
- pickled jalapeños
- baked tortilla chips
- salt and pepper

- Mexican rice (page: 50)
- chopped tomatoes
- fat-free sour cream
- salsa (page: 52)

Method:

1. Prepare rice.
2. Double boil Velveeta cheese until it becomes a sauce while mixing.

3. Top chips with rice and cheese, add onions, tomatoes, salsa, jalapeño rings and sour cream.
4. Salt and pepper to season.

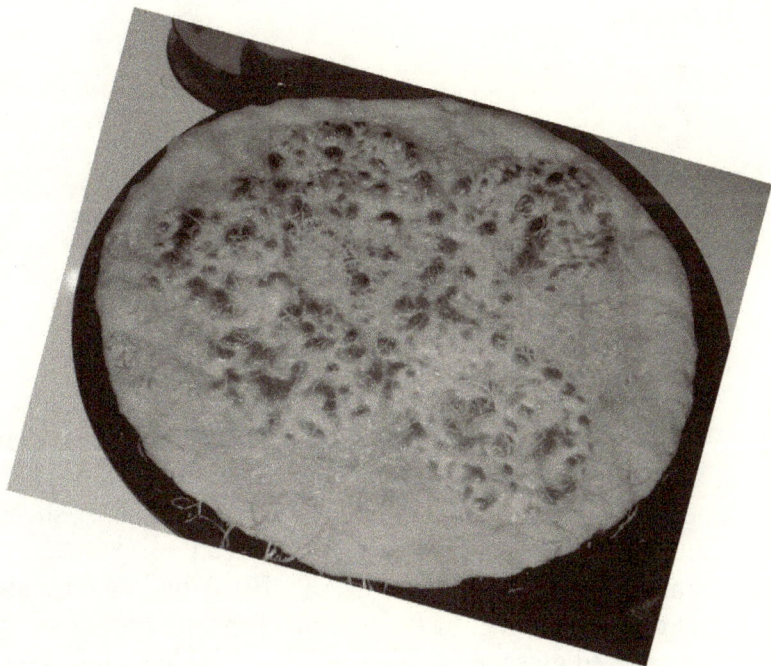

Coca Loca

Coca Loca

Coca is a Spanish flat bread similar to pizza, and can include everything from fruit to meat. This coca is for a basic cheese coca (coca de queso). We call it Coca Loca which translates to "crazy bread" because the kids go absolutely crazy when we make it.

Ingredients:

- 2.5 cups bread flour
- 1 cup + 1 tablespoon of cold water
- 1 packet of rapid rise yeast (2 ¼ teaspoon)
- ½ teaspoon salt
- ½ teaspoon of sugar
- non-stick cooking spray
- low-fat Parmesan cheese
- low fat provolone.

Method:

1. Mix flour, salt and yeast in a bowl. Add water and knead dough for 8-10 minutes.
2. Preheat oven to 200°F, then shut off. Place dough if fat-free sprayed glass or metal bowl and cover with tin-foil.
3. Place in oven for 45 minutes to rise.
4. Place on baking sheet and spread.
5. Brush on low fat butter.
6. Top with provolone
7. Sprinkle with low-fat Parmesan cheese
8. Bake at 450° F for approximately 10 minutes on the middle rack, then an additional 2 on the bottom rack.

Cajun style Dirty Rice

Made with the Holy Trinity of Cajun cooking: celery,
peppers and onions, this traditional Louisiana dish is by
far one of my favorites. Goes great with chicken, or in my
case... as a meal until its own.

Ingredients:

- 1 pound turkey sausage
- 4 cups of chicken broth
- pinch of black pepper
  ¼ teaspoon of chili powder
- 1 teaspoon of red pepper
  flakes
- ¼ teaspoon of paprika

- 2 cups white rice
- ¼ cup green onion diced fine
- ¼ teaspoon of celery salt
- 1 teaspoon of onion powder
- ½ teaspoon of garlic powder

- ¼ teaspoon of salt

Method:

1. Brown sausage in pan.
2. In large sauce pan add meat
   and all ingredients.
3. Bring to a boil.

4. Reduce heat to medium-low,
   cover and cook untouched
   for about 20 minutes.

Dial y Ddraig Nachos (Revenge of The Dragon)

This is not a meal for your average person. This is for those who like it hot. Those who crave the capsaicin , and the raw flavor of fire. It's a buffalo wing nacho of volcanic proportions. A combination of practically every hot flavor you can imagine. A 6-pack of your favorite beer is required to be opened and at the ready by federal law. You've been warned!

Ingredients:

- baked tortilla chips
- 2% light Velveeta cheese product
- non-fat sour cream
- pinch of salt, pepper, and paprika
- 1 pound of boneless, skinless chicken breasts
- Frank's brand hot sauce
- jalapeños
- 1 chopped tomato
- ½ chopped onion

Method:

1. Chop chicken into chunks and cook over medium high heat. Season with salt, pepper, and paprika.
2. Chunk, then double boil cheese on stove top till it forms a sauce.
3. Take cooked chicken and mix with 1-2 cups of Frank's hot sauce.
4. Plate with chips, buffalo chicken, and drizzle with cheese.
5. Top with jalapeños, tomatoes, onions.
6. Garnish with sour cream.

NOSH!

THE INTERNATIONAL DIET COOKBOOK

Desserts, Snacks and Drinks

Liv's Rum Smoothie

Sometimes you need a little something special. Drinking doesn't generally imply healthy, but it can.

Sometime around the 1990's the non-alcoholic smoothie became apart of pop culture as a health fad sold in cafes and supermarkets as a replacement for coffee. Its humble beginnings from Brazil in the 1930's would later get its American reinvention when in the 1970's, Stephen Kuhnau, co-founder of the *Smoothie King*, sold the novelty as a replacement for lactose intolerant milkshake customers such as himself.

Ingredients:
- 1½ ounces of tropical Malibu rum.
- 3½ ounces of strawberry daiquiri mix
- 3 bananas
- ice.

Method:

1. Place in blender.

2. Blend, enjoy.

TRY THIS!

Try adding a couple tablespoons of light peanut butter while blending. It will add some additional fat, but also a lot of protein and great taste!

Boston Cooler

If you've never heard of a Boston Cooler, then you've
probably never spent much time in the Michigan or Ohio
areas of the United States. It's much like a traditional root
beer float, but it uses a regional drink from Detroit's
Boston Boulevard known as Vernors. When I was sick as a
child you drank Vernors. When you were thirsty, you
drank Vernors. When you went to a restaurant but weren't
old enough you drink alcohol, your drank Vernors... and
when you were really good.... you might get a Boston
Cooler.

Ingredients:
- 1 can of diet Vernor's ginger-ale
- 1 scoop of fat-free vanilla ice-cream

Method:
1. Take chilled can of Vernors
   and add 1 scoop of ice
   cream.

2. Enjoy!

QUICK FACTS:
Vernors was invented in 1862 when pharmacist James
Vernor left a medicinal blend of ginger, vanilla and spices
in a oak cask and was called to duty as a soldier in the
American civil war. Four years later, a thirsty, and
surprised Vernor discovered his barrel aged drink had
become the legendary soft-drink which would later be
known as Vernors.

SHOP AROUND:
Search around, most urban areas with major food chains
do have Vernors in the specialty soda section. Shop
around. I've found it in every city I've lived in, but not in
every store.

Chocolate Chip Cookies

These cookies are almost fat-free except for the chocolate. My recipe shaves over 8 grams of fat per cookie in comparison to a typical chocolate chip cookie and guarantees you'll never feel nearly as guilty about eating cookies again.

You can easily replace the chocolate with nuts, fruit or another innovation, but one my personal favorites especially during the holidays is adding mint chocolate chips.

Ingredients:

- 1¾ all purpose flour
- ½ teaspoon baking soda
- ½ cup white sugar
- ¾ cup dark brown sugar
- 1 teaspoon salt
- 1 teaspoon of vanilla extract
- 1/3 cup egg substitute
- ¼ cup of fat free vanilla yogurt
- 11.5 oz. semi-sweet chocolate chunks

Method:

1. Preheat oven to 375° F degrees
2. Mix together the flour, salt, baking soda, sugars.
3. Add yogurt, egg substitute, vanilla and mix.
4. Stir in the chocolate chips.
5. Refrigerate for 5 minutes.
6. Take large spoon sized lumps of cookie dough and place on cookie sheet sprayed with non-fat cooking spray.
7. Bake for approximately 9 minutes.

Cinnatilla Crisp

This is sort of a new take on the churro, a Mexican doughnut. Churros are deep fried, but these can offer a similar taste without the oil. Kid's love them, and you can even take a cookie cutter, and cut them out in shapes before baking making baking them entertaining and interactive as well as great tasting.

Ingredients:

- tortillas
- low-fat light butter or margarine
- cinnamon
- sugar

Method:

1. Brush softened butter onto both sides of tortilla, sprinkle with cinnamon and sugar.

2. Place in preheated 350° F oven for 5-10 minutes or until crispy.

Strawberry Shortcake

Angel food cake is one of the most wonderfully simple foods on this earth. It's fat-free, simple to make, and makes the perfect fat-free dessert when combined with fresh strawberries and non-fat whipped topping. Who says you can't have your cake and eat it too?

You can also add bananas and pineapple for additional flavorings.

Ingredients:

- 1 box of angel food cake prepared per instructions on box
- 2 tubs of fat free whipped topping
- 1 basket of fresh strawberries
- 3 packets of sugar alternative sweetener

Method:

1. Bake cake. Freeze if necessary to cut.

2. Sugar cleaned strawberries and slice.

3. Fill cake with layer of fat free whipped topping and sliced strawberries.

4. Assemble and ice with remaining whipped topping.

5. Garnish with strawberries

Dunks

Basically, a chocolate fondue, this low-fat treat is a
seductive way of treating one's self without having to
forgo the chocolate taste.

Ingredients:

- 1/3 cup Dutch cocoa
- ¼ cup of brown sugar
- ½ cup non-fat buttermilk
- 2 teaspoons of grand Marnier
- bananas
- pineapple
- strawberries.

Method:

1. Combine cocoa and brown sugar, and buttermilk, stir in saucepan over medium heat, begin whisking as temperature rises, then as sugar dissolves (2 minutes.)

2. Remove from heat and add liquor.

3. Pour chocolate sauce in small cups or serve fondue style, and dunk fruit chunks in sauce. Sauce will thicken as it cools.

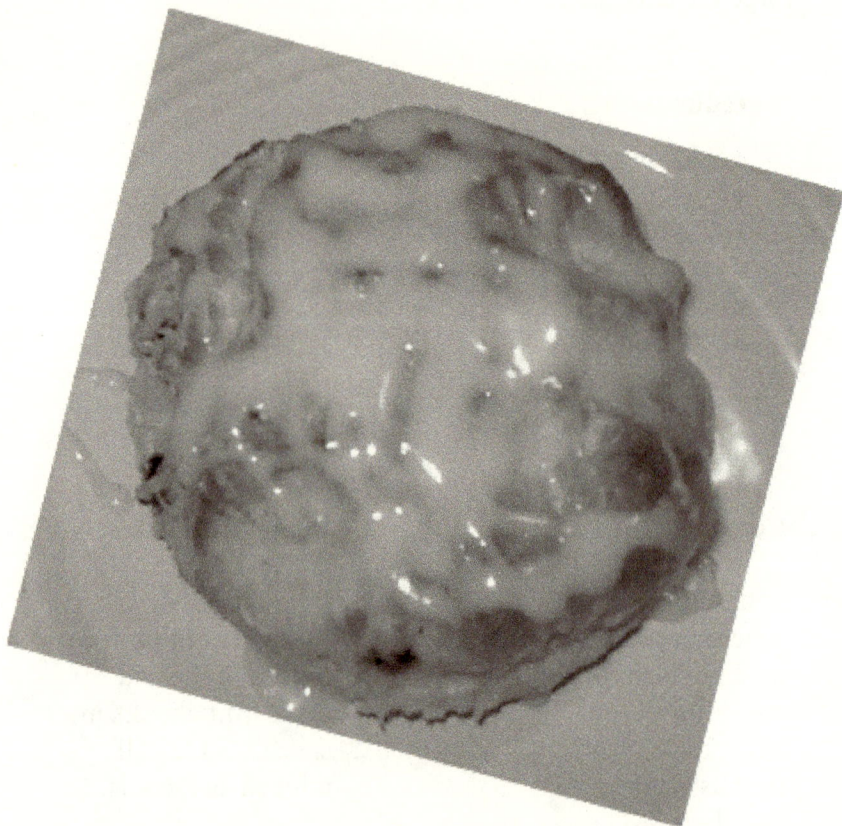

Non-Fat Blueberry Scones

Non-Fat Scones (6 count)

There is nothing like ordering a fresh scone from from a
French bakery in London and topping it with Chantilly
cream. Since America doesn't really have a scone
equivalent, this recipe aims to start a new trend. It's a
blueberry biscuit topped with a sweet glaze. It's a little bit
country, and a lot more rock and roll... best of all, it's
100% delicious.

Ingredients:

Scones:

- 2¼ cups flour (plus additional for dusting)
- 1¼ cups non-fat buttermilk
- 1/3 cup of sugar
- 1 tablespoon baking powder
- 1 teaspoon salt
- ½ teaspoon baking soda
- 1 tablespoon of Butter Buds
- 3 oz of dried blueberries (Mariana brand "wild")

Glaze:

- 1 cup of sifted powdered sugar
- 4 teaspoons of water
- 1 teaspoon of imitation vanilla
- ½ teaspoon of lemon juice

Non-Fat Scones (6 count)

Method:

1. Preheat oven to 450° F.

2. Mix dry ingredients, then stir in buttermilk.

3. Add blueberries, and continue to knead dough adding additional flour as necessary.

4. Move dough to floured cutting board and roll flat to about ¼ - ½ thick (or to desired thickness) and cut approximately 6 scones with a biscuit or cookie cutter.

5. Place in oven and bake for about 8 minutes.

6. Melt 1 tablespoon of low-fat butter or margarine in the microwave, and paint finished biscuits with pastry brush. (optional)

7. Mix glaze ingredients in a bowl, and drizzle over scone with a fork.

Fat-Free Brownies

Fat-free brownies. It's the Holy Grail of baking. A brownie that defies all known forms of scientific law. A delicious, chewy, decadent, even downright naughty brownie which will blow away the minds and mouths of all those who choose to enjoy this eighth world wonder of the world: Liv's fat-free brownies.

Ingredients:

Brownies:

- 1¼ cups flour
- ¼ cup brown sugar
- ¼ teaspoon baking powder
- ½ cup of Hershey's special dark "Dutch" blend cocoa powder

- 1 cup sugar
- 1/3 cup egg substitute
- ¼ teaspoon salt
- 1 6 oz fat free single serving of vanilla yogurt

- 1 teaspoon *vanilla, butter & nut* flavor.

Frosting:

- 8 oz fat free cream cheese
- ½ cup of Hershey's special dark "Dutch" blend cocoa powder

- 3 cups of powdered sugar
- 1 teaspoon vanilla

Method:

1. Mix dry ingredients in bowl with fork.

2. Add wet ingredients and mix till shiny.

3. Bake in 8x8 pan for 25 minutes in a oven preheated to 350° F.

4. Mix all ingredients for frosting with electric mixer, then frost brownies and serve hot and gooey or chill till desired texture is desired.

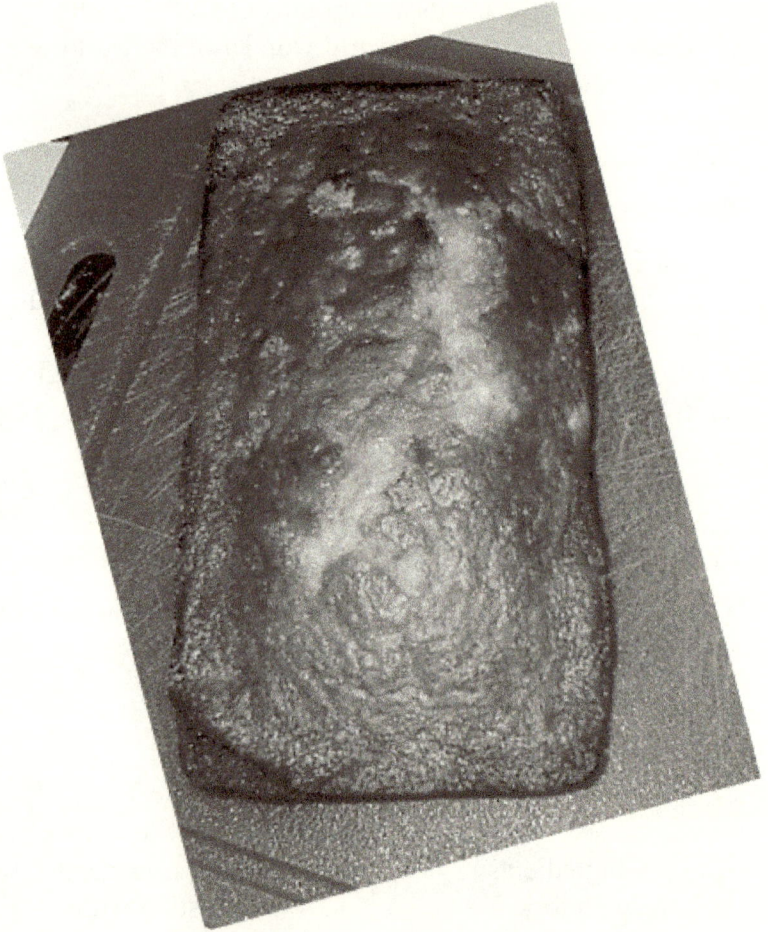

Fat-Free Banana Nutter Bread

Fat-Free Banana Nutter Bread

I grew up on banana nut bread. It's a family favorite, so it only made sense to figure out a way to make it fat-free. It comes out perfectly, and is the most amazing treat as you slice it hot out of the oven.

Ingredients:

- 2 cups wheat flour
- 1 single six ounce cup of fat-free vanilla yogurt
- 1 banana
- ½ teaspoon of baking soda
- ¼ teaspoon of salt
- non-fat cooking spray

- 1 cup sugar
- ½ teaspoon of *vanilla butter, and nut* artificial flavoring
- ¼ cup egg substitute
- ¼ teaspoon cornstarch
- 1 ¼ teaspoon baking powder

Method:

1. Smash banana in bowl.

2. Mix dry ingredients in a bowl, add wet and banana, mix thoroughly.

3. Bake in a 4x8 bread pan sprayed with cooking spray for 350° F in preheated oven for 35-45 minutes or until baked through. Allow to cool for 15 minutes.

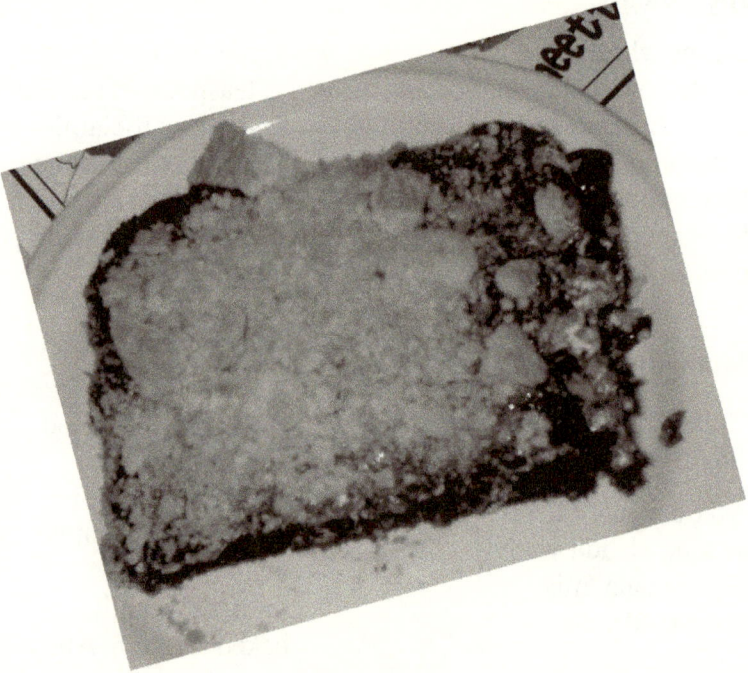

S'more bar

S'more bar

A few years ago we attended a Christmas light show with a friend from the U.K. At the end of the light show, you could purchase stuff to make S'mores over the adjacent outdoor fire in the middle of the park. It was really neat, but apparently in the U.K., S'mores aren't commonplace. Our friend had never had one. We immediately initiated him in this American past-time, and think of him every time we make this recipe or make regular S'mores.

Ingredients:

- brownies in their pan minus frosting (page: 157)
- marshmallow creme
- several graham crackers
- 1/3 cup of Dutch cocoa
- ¼ cup of brown sugar
- 3 tablespoons non-fat buttermilk
- ½ cup powdered sugar

Method:

1. Bake brownies
2. Warm marshmallow creme in microwave for about 30 seconds, and then spread about ½ a jar on top of the brownies.
3. In a sauce pan over medium high heat, mix cocoa, sugars, buttermilk, and continue stirring while bringing to a boil.
4. Quickly remove chocolate frosting from heat and top brownies.
5. Crumble graham cracker on top of of dish.
6. Chill, cut and serve.

Blondies

If you're debating whether to make brownies or cookies, then you might consider a blondie, because that's exactly what you get when you mix the two.

My childhood was filled with a large consumption of blondies from local bakeries in northern Ohio. I can only imagine how many pounds I wouldn't have had to lose if they had made them low-fat like this:

Ingredients:

- 1½ cups of all-purpose flour
- ½ teaspoon of salt
- ½ cup semi-sweet chocolate chips
- ½ cup of white chocolate chips
- non-fat cooking spray

- ½ teaspoon baking powder
- 1½ cups dark brown sugar
- ¼ cup of fat-free vanilla yogurt.
- 1 teaspoon of vanilla extract.
- 1/3 cup of egg substitute

Method:

1. Preheat oven to 350° F
2. Mix dry ingredients.
3. Add wet ingredients, and continue mixing.

4. Spray a 13x9 baking pan with non-fat spray.
5. Transfer mixed batter with spatula and smooth flat.
6. Bake for 18-20 minutes.
7. Allow to cool for 10 minutes.

A Lower Fat White Cake and Cupcake Recipe

First off, this is not a fat-free recipe. It's low fat. While it
does reduce the calories and fat significantly, it does have
low fat butter in it. Special occasions are just that....
special! With that said we cut over 12 grams of fat from
the eggs just by using egg white substitute. That might just
make this your healthiest birthday cake ever.

Makes one 9" pan or twelve cupcakes.

Ingredients:

- 1½ cups of all-purpose flour
- 1 cup of sugar
- ¼ teaspoon of salt

- ¼ cup fat-free vanilla yogurt

- non-fat cooking spray

- 1½ teaspoon baking powder
- ½ cup of egg substitute
- 1 stick of low-fat butter or margarine
- 1½ teaspoon of vanilla extract

Method:

1. Preheat oven to 350° F
2. Sift flour.
3. Mix dry ingredients.
4. Add wet ingredients, and mix with a electronic mixer.
5. Spray baking dish or cupcake papers.
6. Fill pan with batter.
7. For cupcakes, bake 20 minutes or until just slightly golden. Check with a toothpick if done in the middle.
8. Allow to cool.

Cardiff Castle, Wales

Low Fat Welsh Cakes

In Wales, a right of passage is having your mother pass on the family Welsh cake recipe. Made popular by the coal miners of Wales, Welsh cakes, were packed in the miners lunches by their wives. They eventually became popular among everyone, as quick delicious treats, and it was common for the Welsh to whip up a batch from common household ingredients upon a visitor's arrival. In this version we replace the butter with a low fat version and egg substitute that still leave us with a treat reminiscent of the Boom Town coal days.

Ingredients:

- 2 cups of self rising flour
- 1 tablespoon of fat-free milk
- 3/4 cup of sugar
- ½ teaspoon of mixed spice
- 1 stick of low fat butter or margarine.
- 1/3 cup of egg substitute
- 3 oz currants, raisins, etc.

Method:

1. Preheat your stone (or iron skillet) to medium-low (3).

2. Mix all your ingredients in a bowl and then roll into little balls.

3. Flatten out your balls of dough on a floured surface and transfer to pan and cook for about 4 minutes then flip and repeat.

4. Sprinkle a small amount of sugar and serve warm.

*** You also need some non-fat cooking spray.*

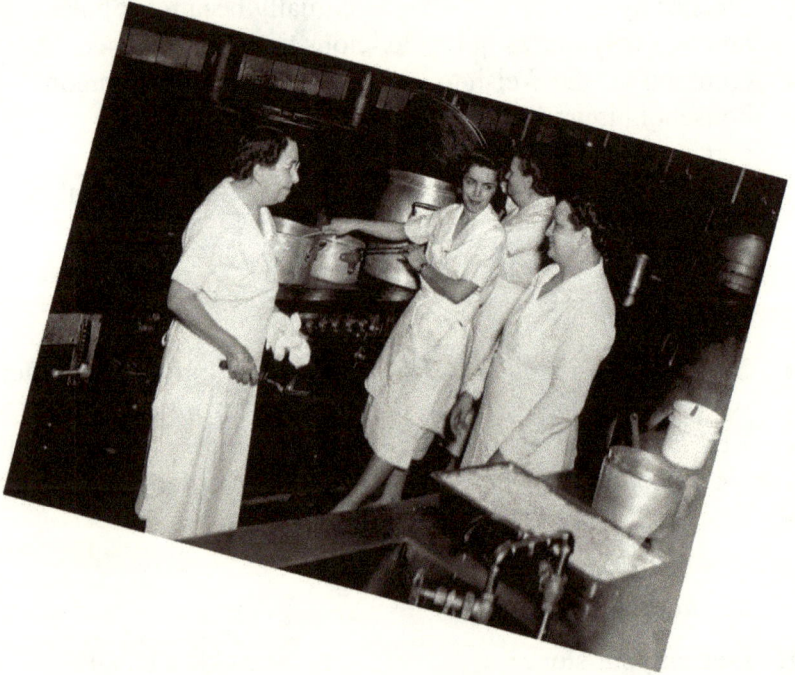

A Family Tradition

Liv's great grandmother, Theresa Schnabel (third from left) worked for eighteen years as a cook with the restaurant for LaSalle & Koch, on Adam Street in Toledo Ohio.

"Even at this moment, as you read this, you are a part of a journey to which you're not aware you're traveling."
-Liv

Share the love and buy a copy for friends or loved ones at:

WWW.NOSHCOOKBOOK.COM

www.ingramcontent.com/pod-product-compliance
Lightning Source LLC
LaVergne TN
LVHW011234080426
835509LV00005B/489